Activities and Bulletins for Everyday Fun

Faye Fredricks, Nell deVries,
and Annetta Dellinger

Cheryl Strikwerda Randall, Illustrator

 Baker Books

A Division of Baker Book House Co
Grand Rapids, Michigan 49516

© 2000 by Baker Book House

Published by Baker Books
a division of Baker Book House Company
P.O. Box 6287, Grand Rapids, MI 49516-6287

Taken from *Children's Bulletin Idea Book* by Faye Fredricks, Nellie deVries, and Annetta Dellinger (1987)

ISBN 0-8010-4448-0

Printed in the United States of America

For current information about all releases from Baker Book House, visit our web site:
http://www.bakerbooks.com

Contents

Guidelines

It is fairly easy to keep children occupied during church services with a few pictures to color or quizzes to complete. But if you want your bulletins to help the children understand the service, make them feel that they are a part of it, and also make them aware of the church family, your bulletins will take on a different perspective.

Involve the pastor as you plan the theme each week. Know what the sermon title is and, if possible, some of the topics that will be covered in the sermon. Check with the choir leader(s) to see if they have any announcements for children. The adult bulletin of the previous week will announce meetings and offerings for the next Sunday. These items can help the children to be aware of church activities.

A very special part of the bulletin will involve the children themselves. Welcoming a new baby or a new family to the church, listing the children who had birthdays that week, mentioning which children are in the hospital, and featuring a mystery child are ways to make children feel that they have a bulletin designed especially for them. The mentioning of children's names creates an interest that cannot be duplicated elsewhere. Ask the children to prepare cards for those who are sick. Have them pray for special needs and thank God for answers to prayers.

You may want to ask the children to design a cover for special days or prepare a puzzle or quiz. Jokes and riddles can occasionally be included also.

But the most important thing is the sermon topic. Be creative in the ways to involve children in listening. Perhaps a fill-in quiz or a list of words to listen for will help. You may want to refer to hymns or anthems the congregation or choirs will be singing. Try to keep the theme of the day in mind. Sometimes that is impossible; then a "generic" or "ready-to-use" bulletin may be the answer.

Now that your goals are established, you're ready to decide who will prepare the bulletin. You may want to ask one person to have the sole responsibility. This can also be worked out well by a committee, provided one or two members have the assignment for a specified block of time. Rotate the months so that the same people are not always responsible for the same special days, such as Easter or Thanksgiving. Perhaps you have volunteered or have been appointed. Enthusiasm, creativity, and a sensitivity to children and the purpose of worship are the key ingredients for the editor(s) of a church bulletin.

Use the grids we've prepared to lay out the bulletin. A local printer can prepare copies of the grid in nonreproducing blue ink. Type and drawings can easily be placed on the blue lines, and the lines will not show on the completed bulletin. The grids make it so much easier to get a neat bulletin. Use rubber cement to paste. It is easy to use and clean up.

How should the bulletin be laid out? There should be a careful balance between a set format for easy recognition and good variety for interest. A logo or design featuring the name of your church (Millbrook Morning Glories) is a good idea.

Typewriter type tends to be a little stilted for children but can be used to give directions. Hand lettering works well. Children love to color in outline letters or fill in missing spaces in the letters. The grids will help avoid lettering that is poorly spaced or crooked.

For more ideas, exchange bulletins with neighboring churches or comb the activity book section of a bookstore. Be sure to follow copyright restrictions. Some publishers will allow local church use without charge. Avoid using greeting cards, comics, or children's page items from a local newspaper. That material is covered by stringent copyright laws. So is coloring book art.

Assemble your materials into a workable filing system. The first section should be a "Current Week Information" file. It could contain items such as last week's adult bulletin (for upcoming events), offering schedule, pastor's preaching schedule, information on contact persons (choir director, church school leader). You may wish to include a file for each of the following:

Announcements
   Birth
   Birthday

Library
Music
Baptism
Basic Truths
Bible
Catechism (Heidelberg or Westminster)
Church Year
Advent
Christmas
Epiphany
Lent
Easter
Ascension Day
Pentecost
Cross References (Ideas/Bible verses)
Fruit of the Spirit
Holidays
Valentine's Day
Mother's Day
Memorial Day
Father's Day
Fourth of July
Labor Day
Thanksgiving Day
Lord's Supper
New Testament
Offerings
Old Testament
Parables
Prayer
Profession of Faith
Puzzles
Quizzes
Seasons, Nature
Special Days
Hunger Awareness
Mission Emphasis
Reformation Day
Supplies
Borders

Expressive pictures
General pictures
Grid paper
Trim
Ten Commandments
Worship

Children love to be involved in bulletin preparation and distribution. Choose one or two to be assistant editors and rotate the assignment. The assistant editors can help plan the contents, select the borders, arrange the art, and, under your supervision, do the layout. Be sure to list the names of the assistant editors in the bulletins they prepare. Select children (alphabetically is a good system) to distribute the bulletins to children of the congregation as they arrive on Sunday morning; list their names in the bulletin too.

Allow for additional activities in bulletins occasionally. Include extra paper so cards or letters can be prepared. Arrange for handy collection of the items and be sure to thank the children for making them. That is an excellent way to remember sick, shut-ins, senior citizens, the pastor, and even the president or prime minister.

The church family corner can be a meaningful introduction to the practice of caring about fellow members. List prayer concerns and invite children to make a card or draw a picture for the people involved. The "mystery person" feature is an excellent way to introduce the shy child or the quiet one who is usually overlooked. Offer a prize (a bookmark) to the first person to correctly identify the mystery person and also give a bookmark to the mystery person. Often the mystery corner is the first item checked by the children. Be sure to credit both the puzzle solver and the mystery person in the next week's bulletin.

Occasionally you may wish to insert a bookmark or other advertising material distributed by the agency for which the offering is being given. A picture of a missionary family, especially if it includes their children, is a good way to create interest in missions.

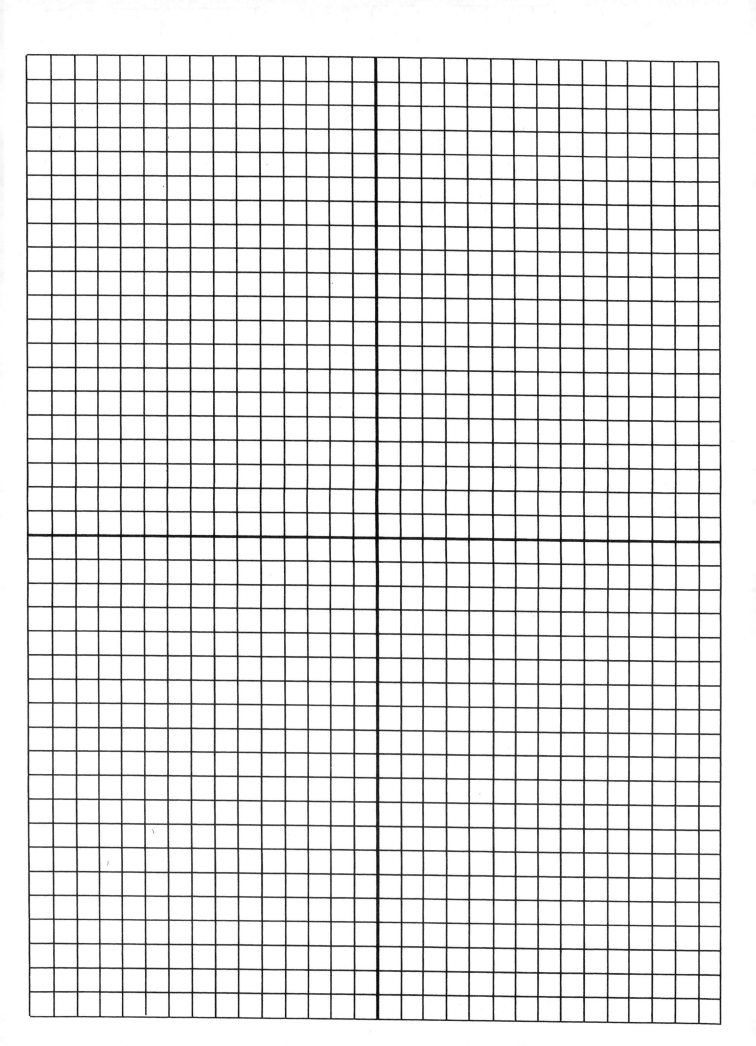

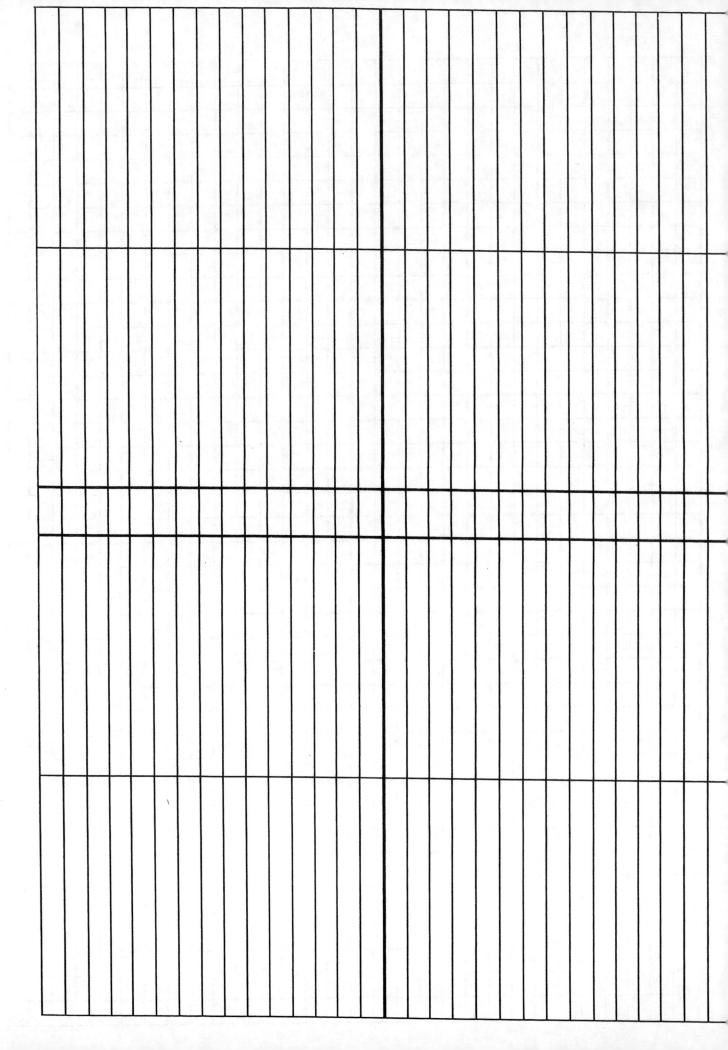

Ready-to-Use Bulletins

Connect the dots to find a picture of someone who thanked God long ago.

CHILDREN'S BULLETIN
THANKSGIVING

The fourth Thursday in November is proclaimed by the President of the United States to be a Day of Thanksgiving to God by the people of our nation. God really has blessed our country. As Christians we always thank God for His goodness. List one of God's gifts to you on each of the tail feathers of the turkey on this bulletin cover.

Two ways to draw turkeys:

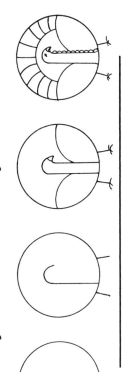

Trace around your hand. Add the legs and feet to the bottom.

Turn the thumb into a head by an eye, a bill and a wavy line to the neck.

Try these at home!

	T		
2	H	A	N
3			K
4			S

Fill in the blanks with the correct words.

1. "Thanks be to God for his indescribable _____." (2 Corinthians 9:15)

2. "Thanks and _____ . . . be to our God." (Revelation 7:12)

3. "We always thank God . . . when we _____ for you." (Colossians 1:3)

4. "I thank Christ Jesus . . . who has given me _____." (1 Timothy 1:12)

5. "For this reason I _____ before the Father." (Ephesians 3:14)

6. "Give thanks to him and _____ his name." (Psalm 100:4b)

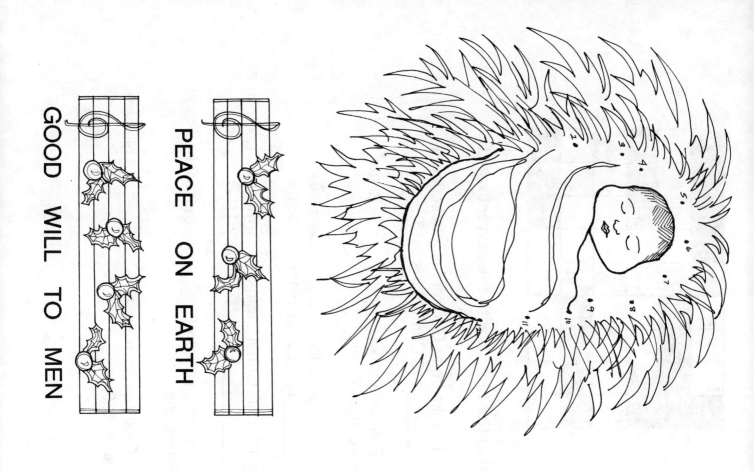

PEACE ON EARTH

GOOD WILL TO MEN

CHILDREN'S BULLETIN

MERRY CHRISTMAS!

Christmas

The very first Christmas gift was from God.
That Gift was His Son, Jesus.

Draw a picture of baby Jesus.
Next, draw you beside the baby.

THE BIRTH OF JESUS
Matthew 2:1–18; Luke 2:40–52

Draw a line from the names
below to the correct statement.

CAESAR AUGUSTUS   City where Jesus was born.

JOSEPH   Mother of Jesus.

NAZARETH   City where Joseph and Mary lived.

BETHLEHEM   He said the world should be taxed.

MARY   They followed a star.

SHEPHERDS   He held Jesus in the temple and praised God.

ANGEL   Visited Jesus in the stable.

SIMEON   Joseph, Mary and Jesus fled to this place.

ANNA   Means savior.

JESUS   Brought the message of Jesus' birth.

WISE MEN   The king who wanted to kill Jesus.

EGYPT   Husband of Mary.

HEROD   City where Jesus was brought to the temple.

JERUSALEM   An old prophetess who saw the baby Jesus.

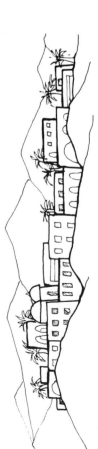

Women in the Bible

Search for Bible wives:

```
Z A O P B S R E H T O M S A R A H R T L
P R I S C I L L A U C P S D W H A E E E
S W E J A B I G A I L E V E A T N H F A
E H G E V P E L I T N E G K I U N T J J
V A K Z I P P O R A H L E M P R A S N M
I L L E A H O H T T P B A T H S H E B A
W G P B B Z O H I Q E L I Z A B E T H R
S E T E L E H C A R U D E B E H C O J Y
V M I L C A H W X N A O M I C H A L Y A
```

Abigail
Eglah
Eve
Jezebel
Mary
Naomi
Rebekah
Sarah

Asenath
Elizabeth
Hannah
Jochebed
Micah
Priscilla
Ruth
Zipporah

Bathsheba
Esther
Jael
Leah
Michal
Rachel
Sapphira

PICTURE STUDY

Match each picture to a Bible verse. Each picture means something special in the story of Esther.

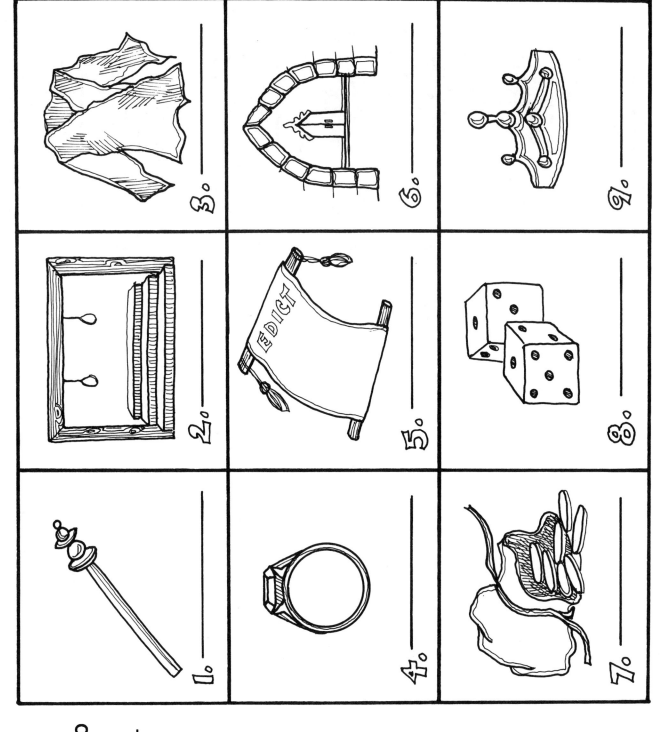

1. _____

2. _____

3. _____

4. _____

5. _____

6. _____

7. _____

8. _____

9. _____

Esther 4:1–3

Esther 5:2

Esther 8:1–2

Esther 5:9–13

Esther 7:10

Esther 2:17

Esther 3:12–14

Esther 3:7

Esther 3:8–9

FAMILIES

Our families are very important.

In our families, God shows us His special care.

Let's thank Him for our families right now.

Dear God, Thank You for our families and for Your special care for us. For Jesus' sake, Amen.

CHILDREN'S BULLETIN

GOD KEEP YOU IN HIS CARE

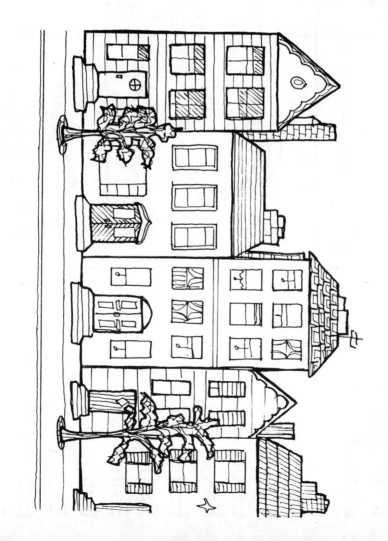

God really does care for His people. And not just adults only. One day, when His disciples chased the children away because they thought that Jesus was too busy, He said to them, "Don't do that! Let the children come to me, for my kingdom belongs to them!"

Johnny cares for his puppy too! He wants to find him. Can you help?

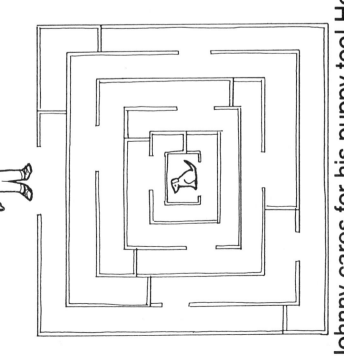

When bad things happened to Job, he questioned if God still cared for him. The answer was always Yes. God always cares for His people.

And He will always care for you too!

Find the hidden words from Job 1

```
          R
      B   H   B
  D   O   G   N   P
Q R J F E A V
B S O X E N R E S
  V L H B C H O
    S A T A N
      H S E
        A
```

God
Lord
Sheep

Job
Oxen
Satan

Put the letters in **Prayer** in order in the boxes below.

Monday
☐ ray for the hungry people today.

Tuesday
☐ emember to pray and read your Bible today.

Wednesday
☐ prayer for our church should be raised today.

Thursday
☐ our family needs your prayers today.

Friday
☐ ven if you're busy, take time to pray today.

Saturday
☐ emember to thank God today for all the blessings of the week.

CHILDREN'S BULLETIN

PRAYER

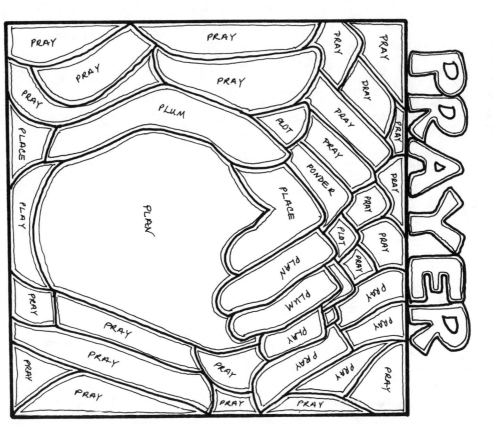

Color all the spaces with the word "pray" in them.

Dial-a-Verse to see what God tells us in 1 Thessalonians 5:17.

Let your fingers do the walking . . . .

The first # under a line tells you what # to look at on the dial. The 1, 2, or 3 tells you what letter you need in that circle on the dial. Example: 6-2=N. Get it? HAPPY DIALING!

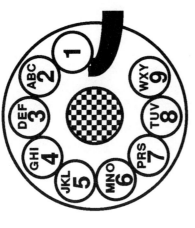

"_____ _____ _____ _____
2-3 6-3 6-2 8-1 4-3 6-2 8-2 2-1 5-3 9-3   7-1 7-2 2-1 9-3 "

Do you know any other verses about prayer?

_____

_____

_____

PRAYER is TALKING WITH GOD

Never busy
Call day or night
No number to look up
Never put on "hold"
Person to person
Not long distance
Private line

List some things you would like to talk to God about today.

Draw a picture of something you like to do in the snow.

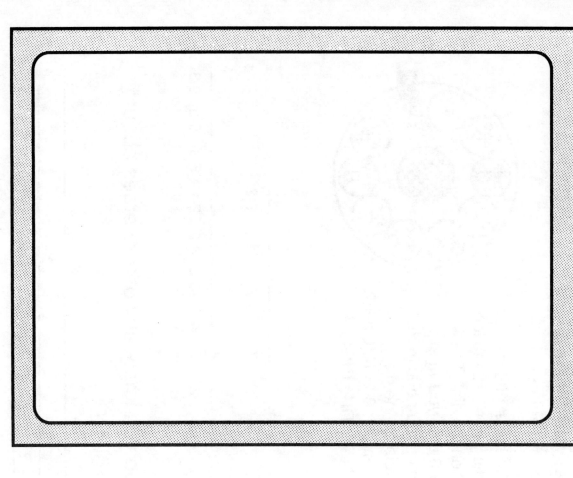

CHILDREN'S BULLETIN

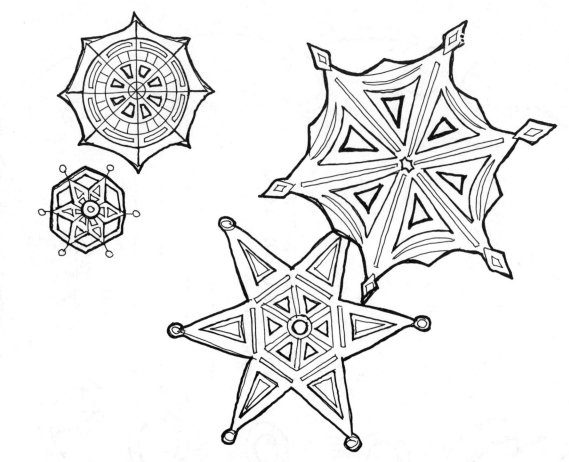

Thank God for snowflakes!

Winter

Every snowflake is different, just like people. That's what makes things special!

Draw some more snowflakes. Make each one different. Draw a picture of your family.

MY FAMILY

God tells us how He wants us to love in two greatest commandments.

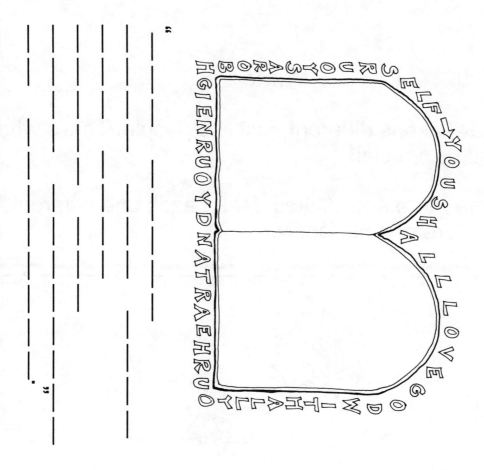

SELF→YOU SHALL LOVE GOD WITH ALL YOUR HEART AND YOUR NEIGHBOR AS YOURSELF

Start at the arrow and write the message on the lines below the tablets.

" _____ _____ _____ _____ _____ _____

_____ _____ _____ _____ _____ _____

_____ _____ _____ _____ _____ _____

_____ _____ _____ _____ _____ _____

_____ _____ _____ ."

CHILDREN'S BULLETIN

Valentine's Day

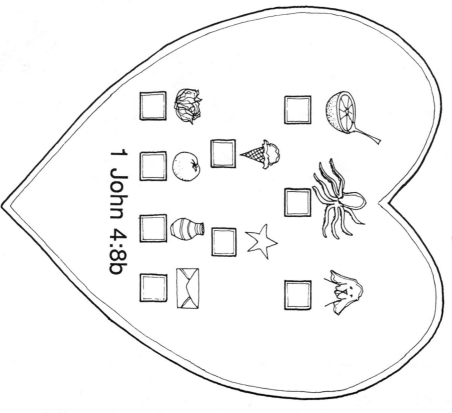

1 John 4:8b

Put the first letter of each object in the box below it. Then read the lines below the tablets.

Valentine Match-Up

Match up each big valentine with a small one to see where the verse is found in the Bible.

CHILDREN'S BULLETIN

New Life in Christ

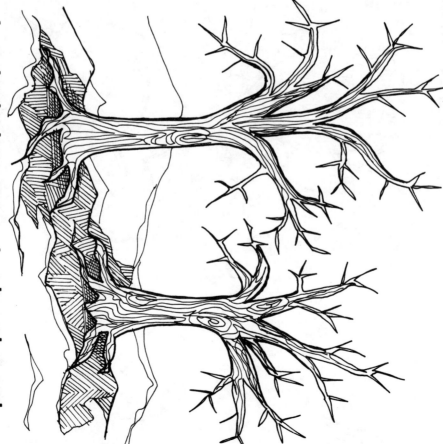

In spring buds appear on tree branches and soon they seem to spring to life again. Make these winter trees come to life with lots of leaves.

GOD TURNED THIS LOWLY

INTO A BEAUTIFUL _____

*His love can change you too.

Just as a caterpillar changes into a beautiful butterfly
we can have a new life in Christ. We change!

DEAR REV AND MRS
JONES,
HOW ARE YOU?
HOW THINGS
ARE WELL ON THE
GOING WEL ON FISH
MISSION
HONDURA
INTERE

Look at each picture. Put a C (for caterpillar) in the circle if it's something we would do
as our old self. Put a B (for butterfly) if it's something our new selves might do.

Activities
and Cover Ideas

CHRISTMAS WORD PUZZLE

December—it's Christmas! So look in this rhyme
for words that are hidden in letters and lines. Up,
down, and crosswise, go side to side, for thirty-
three words are trying to hide!

<u>Mistletoe</u>, <u>holly</u>, <u>Nativity</u>, <u>star</u>,
<u>Gifts</u>, <u>bells</u>, and <u>swaddling</u>, <u>candle</u> and <u>cards</u>,
<u>Mary</u> and <u>Joseph</u>, <u>baby</u> and <u>manger</u>,
<u>Stable</u>, <u>poinsettia</u>, <u>Wise Men</u> and <u>shepherds</u>,

<u>Bethlehem</u>, <u>wreath</u>, <u>Jerusalem</u>, <u>carols</u>,
<u>Santa Claus</u>, <u>church</u>, <u>ivy</u> and <u>angel</u>,
<u>Greens</u>, <u>boughs</u>, and <u>tree</u>, <u>sleigh</u> and <u>deer</u>,
Then <u>chime</u> to tell us that <u>Christmas</u> is here!

```
C A R O L S Y R A M E H E L H T E B
H C R U H C T G D E C E M B E R Q A
R Z L P R J L R A N Z S H G U O B
I S J K R F V T I M N E M E S I W Y
S N L M T O I T S H E P H E R D S V
T E F S L J T M I S T L E T O E L I
M E R W R E A T H O L C A N D L E H
A R A T S A N T A C L A U S S Q I P
S G G N I N K K M A N G E R U Z G E
E M I H C G D E E R J K R Q R R H S
H O L L Y E S W A D D L I N G S E O
P R I B E L L S J S T A B L E L K J
```

CHRISTMAS CAROL CROSSWORD

1. Ring the _____
2. Once in _____ David's City
3. O Leave Your _____
4. O Come All _____ Faithful
5. Joy to the _____
6. _____ Night
7. What Can I _____ Him?
8. Away in a _____
9. Bethlehem _____ Sleeping
10. Go Tell It on the _____

Word Bank
World
Silent
Manger
Bells
Sheep
Give
Mountain
Lay
Ye
Royal

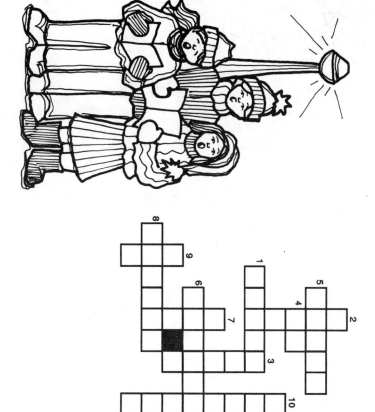

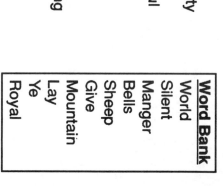

Transfiguration Word Search

Find these words from Mark 9:1–8:

Jesus, Peter, James, John, Elijah, Moses, mountain, white, cloud, voice, shelters, son, love, enveloped, alone

```
B P Q S V O I C E F
T E S R E T L E H S
H T L M R U C G B W
G E V O N Y L I W M
A R J S V B O Y A O
P D H E W E U C I U
K E A S D Z D V A N
P P W C K J P L J T
J O H E G L O R Y A
A L I M R N F H X I
M E T N E Y R K N N
E V E L I J A H N P
S N K I N G D O M S
O E Z C J E S U S M
```

Fill in the letters using the code below.

Tr __(5)__ ly __(3)__ s __(1)__ y t __(4)__ y __(4)__ __(5)__ ,

th __(2)__ r __(2)__ r __(1)__ s __(4)__ m __(2)__

st __(1)__ nd __(3)__ ng h __(2)__ r __(2)__ wh __(4)__ w __(3)__ ll

n __(4)__ t t __(1)__ st __(2)__ d __(2)__ __(1)__ th b __(2)__ f __(4)__ r __(2)__

th __(2)__ y s __(2)__ __(2)__ th __(1)__ t th __(2)__

k __(3)__ ngd __(4)__ m __(4)__ f G __(4)__ d h __(1)__ s

c __(4)__ m __(2)__ w __(3)__ th p __(4)__ w __(2)__ r.

M __(1)__ rk 9:1 RSV

a = 1   e = 2   i = 3

o = 4   u = 5

Draw pictures of four needs you might pray for.

Connect the dots in each square.

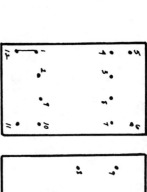

Now draw a picture of a happy boy or girl.

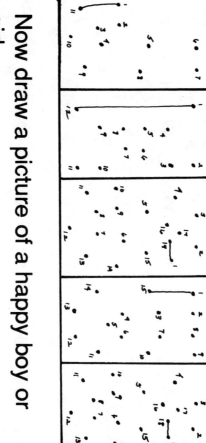

Start at the dot and find the five names of Jesus.

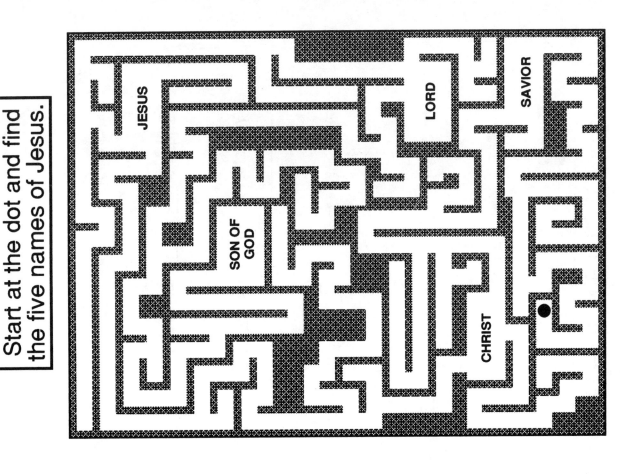

JESUS
LORD
SAVIOR
SON OF GOD
CHRIST

G 😀 L 😊 M 😊 A 😊 R 😊

H 😀 I 😊 F 😊 E 😊 O 😊

T 😐 D 😊 W 😊

Use the code to find out what Jesus said about Himself.
Then read John 8:12.

THE TEN COMMANDMENTS

1
You shall have no other _____ before me.

2
You shall not _____ for yourself an _____.

3
You shall not misuse the _____ of the _____ your God.

4
Remember the _____ day by keeping it _____.

5
Honor your _____ and your _____.

6
You shall not _____.

7
You shall not commit _____.

8
You shall not _____.

9
You shall not give false _____ against your _____.

10
You shall not _____ your neighbor's _____. You shall not covet your neighbor's wife, or his _____ or maidservant, his _____ or donkey, or anything that belongs to your _____.

Exodus 20:3–17

Jesus gave us two important commandments. Read them to yourself. Then find the
underlined words in the square.

"<u>Love</u> the <u>Lord</u> with all your <u>heart</u>, with all
your <u>soul</u>, with all your <u>mind</u>, and with all
your <u>strength</u>.
The <u>second</u> most important command-
ment is this: Love your <u>neighbor</u> as you love
<u>yourself</u>."

see Mark 12:30–31

```
I X S E C O N D Q U E K
M N L S Z G O D F Z T F
P E Q O F D N I M N L L
O I U V Z U E E X Z E
R G Z L Y E G M G A Q S
T H H J Z F D X L L V R
A B R E K N Q J O L I U
N O G D A X Q N R N K O
T R L M K R X L D T Q Y
P Z M D Q J T F Z G Z X
Q O R X S T R E N G T H
C B Q E E H Q Z X K J H
```

GOD'S RULES FOR US

This is number ____

Do not ___ ___ ___ ___ ___ i ___ ___   to get
              36 12   44 32   24 16

of ___ a ___ ___ ___ ___ o ___ ___   to
    40   36 12 24 8   20 24 8

___ ___ e ___ ___ ___ ___ e ___ ___   that
36 12   4 36 12   28 32

___ o ___ ___ ___ .
36   12 28 32

Each number stands for a letter. Write
the letters in the spaces.

4 = b	28 = r
8 = g	32 = s
12 = h	36 = t
16 = k	40 = w
20 = l	44 = y
24 = n	

Q. If there is only one God, why do we talk about three?

A. If you have faith in the *true God*, you believe in God the Father, God the Son, and God the Holy Spirit.

Here is 1 apple. The apple has 3 parts.

The 3 parts of the apple have different purposes:

The peel

__16__ __18__ __15__ __20__ __5__ __3__ __20__ __19__ .

It keeps the apple healthy.

The flesh of the apple is good to

__16__ __5__ __12__   __6__ __12__ __5__ __19__ __8__   __3__ __15__ __18__ __5__ .

The core of the apple contains

__5__ __1__ __20__ .

__19__ __5__ __5__ __4__ __19__   from which apple trees grow.

THE APPLE HAS 3 PARTS BUT YOU KNOW YOU DON'T HAVE 3 APPLES—JUST 1.

A	B	C	D	E	F	G	H	I	J	K	L	M
1	2	3	4	5	6	7	8	9	10	11	12	13

N	O	P	Q	R	S	T	U	V	W	X	Y	Z
14	15	16	17	18	19	20	21	22	23	24	25	26

THERE IS ONLY 1 TRUE GOD.

The 1 true God has 3 persons:
GOD THE FATHER,
GOD THE SON,
GOD THE HOLY SPIRIT

The 3 persons of the 1 true God have different purposes.

God the Father is our

__3__ __18__ __5__ __1__ __20__ __15__ __18__ .

God the Son is our

__19__ __1__ __22__ __9__ __15__ __18__ .

God the Holy Spirit makes us

__8__ __15__ __12__ __25__ .

The 3 main ways we can know God is the

Father, ✝ the **Son,** and the **Holy Spirit.**

Find 3 of each of these symbols in the picture.

PUT ON THE FULL ARMOR OF GOD

Below is a list of the spiritual weapons that God has given us. Can you put each one in its correct place on the man of armor on the opposite page?

Truth

Righteousness

The gospel of peace

Faith

Salvation

The Spirit, which is the Word of God

(Answer: Ephesians 6:14–17)

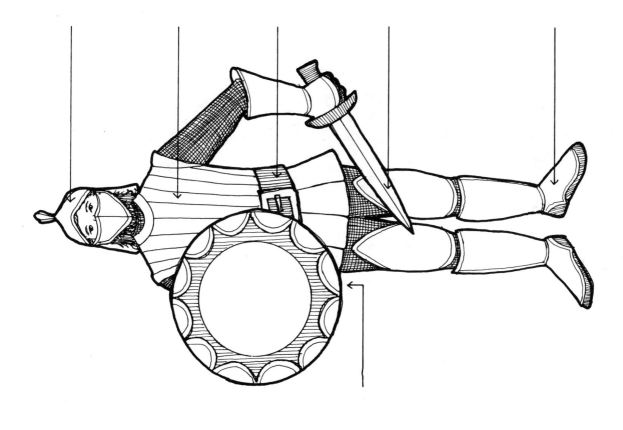

STAND FIRM THEN!

Remember Who You Are

Isaiah 49:1

We Are God's Covenant People

Look at your fingertips. Do you see anything? Are they smooth? If you put ink on one and pressed it on a piece of paper, you would see many little lines. This is called a fingerprint. You can't see them, but fingerprints identify us.

God's people have something that identify them, too. They have been baptized with *water* to identify them as God's covenant people.

Can you make these fingerprints into some *covenant people?*

Use these prints to make some interesting creatures.

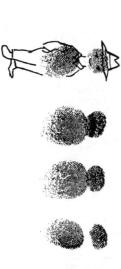

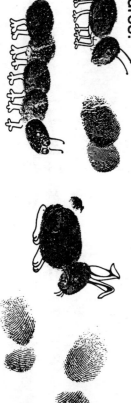

Let your fingers do the walking . . .

The first # under a line tells you what # to look at on the dial. The 1, 2, or 3 tells you what letter you need in that circle on the dial. Example: 6-2=N.
Get it? HAPPY DIALING!

Providence means

___ ___ ___   ___ ___ ___
7-1 7-2 6-3   4-1 6-3 3-1

___ ___ ___ ___ ___ ___
8-3 4-3 3-1 3-2 7-3

The butterfly is a sign of new life. It changes from a caterpillar to a butterfly through a beautiful plan of God. Saul changed from a sinner to a saint through the grace of God and so can we! Draw a butterfly to remind you of that.

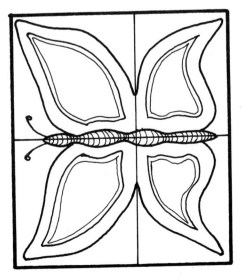

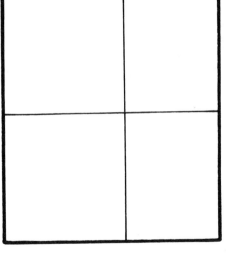

Q. Is it fair that God asks us to be perfect when it's impossible for us?

A. Line 1 Y E S O N E B E C A U S E F O U R H E
Line 2 M A D E Y E S U S N O P E R F E C T
Line 3 S O U L M A N R U I N E D I T B O D Y
Line 4 R E D W H E N B L U E A D A M G O L D
Line 5 A B C S A I B N C N A E B D C A B C A

Our sins *must* be paid for!

To find our answer follow these instructions:

Cross out the 2 *number* words in Line 1.
Cross out the *answer* words in Line 2. (Yes/No)
Cross out the first four and the last four letters in Line 3.
Cross out the 3 *color* words in Line 4.
Cross out all of the *A's, B's & C's* in Line 5.

Q. Will God let sin go unpunished?
A. No! Dial-a-Verse to see what Paul tells us in Romans 6:23.

$\overline{3\text{-}3}$ $\overline{6\text{-}3}$ $\overline{7\text{-}2}$ $\overline{8\text{-}1}$ $\overline{4\text{-}2}$ $\overline{3\text{-}2}$ $\overline{9\text{-}1}$ $\overline{2\text{-}1}$ $\overline{4\text{-}1}$ $\overline{3\text{-}2}$ $\overline{7\text{-}3}$

$\overline{6\text{-}3}$ $\overline{3\text{-}3}$ $\overline{7\text{-}3}$ $\overline{4\text{-}3}$ $\overline{6\text{-}2}$ $\overline{4\text{-}3}$ $\overline{7\text{-}3}$

$\overline{3\text{-}1}$ $\overline{3\text{-}2}$ $\overline{2\text{-}1}$ $\overline{8\text{-}1}$ $\overline{4\text{-}2}$

Let your fingers do the walking . . . .

The first # under a line tells you what # to look at on the dial. The 1, 2, or 3 tells you what letter you need in that circle on the dial. Example: 6-2=N. Get it? HAPPY DIALING!

God was unhappy with all the sin in the world, so He decided to send a flood. He saw that Noah was a good man.

God told Noah to build a huge boat and to put 2 of every kind of animal in it. People laughed at Noah, but Noah trusted God. He knew that God would take care of his family. We, too, must trust that God knows what's best for us, and that He will take care of us.

Find 10 animals hiding from Noah. Then color the picture.

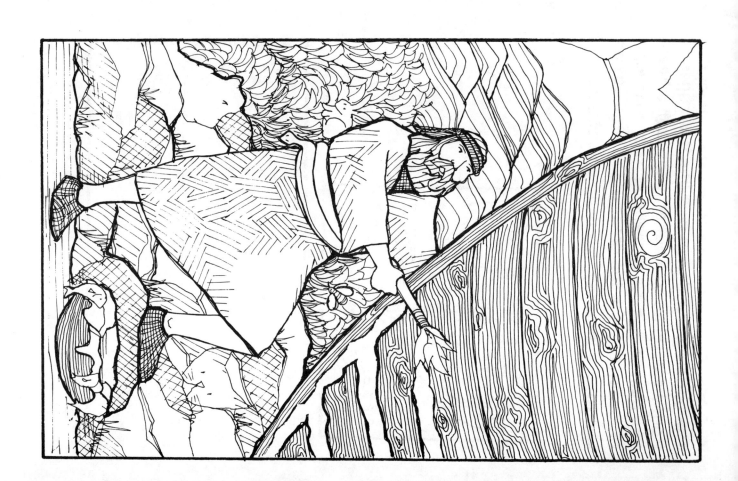

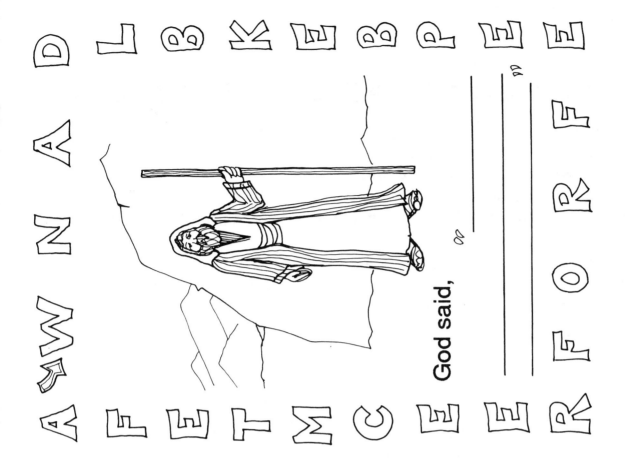

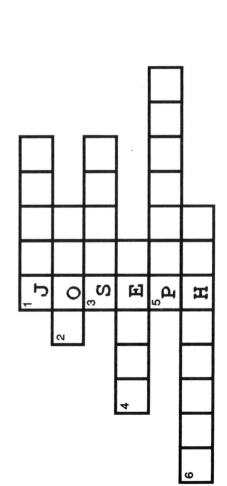

Start at the **W** and write down every other letter to see our verse from Genesis 17. Color in the picture of Abraham.

God said, "___ ___ ___"

Put one letter in each box to finish this puzzle. The passages are all from Genesis.

1. Joseph's father (49:1)

2. Joseph had a beautiful _____ (37:3).

3. There were _____ years of prosperity and _____ years of famine (41:29–30).

4. Joseph interpreted the cupbearer's and the _____'s dream (40:16).

5. He made Joseph second-in-command of all Egypt (41:39–40).

6. He was Joseph's first master (39:1).

1. J
2. O
3. S
4. E
5. P
6. H

Daniel and the Feast of Belshazzar

Daniel 5

King Belshazzar made a great feast.
Many people came to the feast.
They drank wine from the gold cups that had come from God's temple in
     Jerusalem.
They drank wine and praised false gods.
Then a hand was seen writing a message on the wall.
Daniel was able to tell the meaning of the message.
King Belshazzar did not fear God.
That night he died.

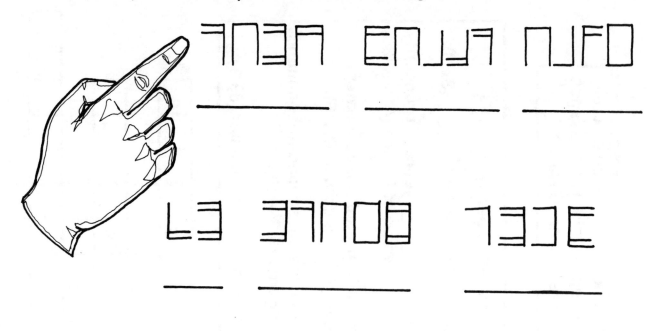

Using the key above, decipher the coded message below.

_____ _____ _____

DANIEL IN THE LIONS' DEN

Daniel 6

Below is a one-way crossword puzzle to solve. All the clues are in verse 10.
Write the answers in the verse below and then in the puzzle squares.

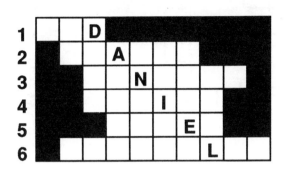

"Now when (4)_____ learned that
the decree had been published, he
went home to his upstairs room where
the (3) _____ opened toward
(6) _____. (5) _____ times
a day, he got down on his knees and
(2) _____, giving thanks to his
(1) _____, just as he had done before."

The answers to this part are found in verses 21 and 22.

(7)" _____ answered, (8)' ___
_____, live forever! (6) ___ _____
sent his (4) _____, and he (5) _____
the mouths of the (1) _____. They
have (3) _____ _____ me, because I
was found innocent in his sight. Nor have
(2) ___ ever _____ any wrong
before you, O king.' "

STACK-A-WORD*
2 Kings 7:1–20

ACROSS
Camp
Elisha
Four
Measure
Shekels
Syrians
Kings

UP & DOWN
Barley
Famine
Lepers
Prophecy
Samaria
Tents

*The number of squares will give you a clue to how many letters in a word.

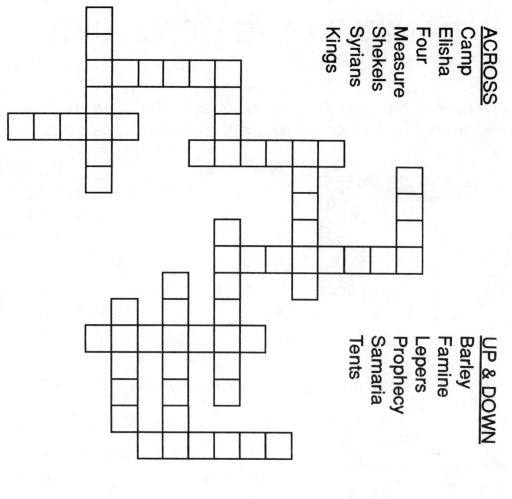

Use the names of these Bible People to finish this puzzle . . .

Bible People

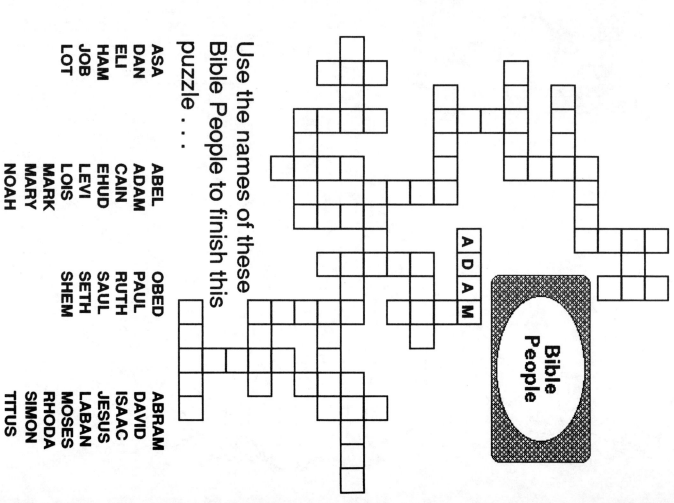

ABEL
ADAM
CAIN
EHUD
LEVI
LOIS
MARK
MARY
NOAH

ASA
DAN
ELI
HAM
JOB
LOT

OBED
PAUL
RUTH
SAUL
SETH
SHEM

ABRAM
DAVID
ISAAC
JESUS
LABAN
MOSES
RHODA
SIMON
TITUS

GIVE ME FIVE!

Write the name of a Bible character whose name starts with each of these first five letters of the alphabet.

A _____

B _____

C _____

D _____

E _____

Name 5 books of the Old Testament.

1. _____

2. _____

3. _____

4. _____

5. _____

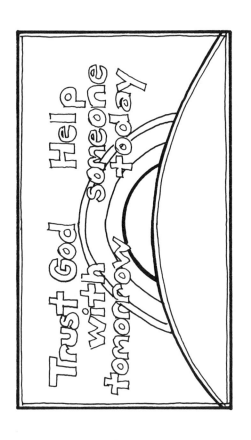

Trust God   Help
    with someone
    tomorrow   today

Below is a verse about trusting in God. Fill in the missing letters in the words by matching the shapes of the boxes.

TR⬡ST ⬦N TH⬦
L⬜RD W⬦TH ⬦LL
TH⬡N⬡ H⬡ART

Proverbs 3:5 KJV

CHILDREN'S BULLETIN

God Sent His _____!

Draw-in Pictures

A robin is a sign
of spring.
Give him a bill so
he can sing.

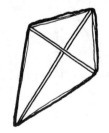

Through the air this
kite will sail,
if you will add a
fancy tail.

Draw one curved line,
if you would try,
to help keep someone
nice and dry.

Into the garden
fall spring showers.
Would you like to
draw the flowers?

RUN THE
RACE!

HELP THIS RUNNER TO THE FINISH LINE

FINISH

Fill in this verse:

" _____ shall _____

the Lord your _____ and

_____ only shall you _____

" Matthew 4:10 RSV

What does it mean to be a Christian?

To find part of what it means to be a Christian first do the math problems. Write the answers in the box right below the problem. Now look at the code below to see what letter that number stands for. Write that letter in the box below the number.

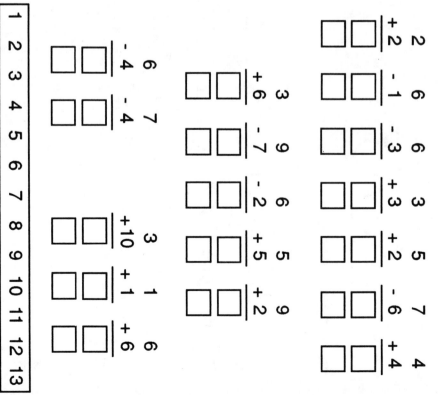

	2 +2	6 -1	6 -3	3 +3	5 +2	7 -6	4 +4

	3 +6	9 -7	6 -2	5 +5	1 +1	9

	6 -4	7 -4	3 +10	6 +6

1	2	3	4	5	6	7	8	9	10	11	12	13
a	o	n	c	e	t	r	l	f	u	s	d	g

God's House

We usually treat our houses in a special way.

The church is God's house, and we want to treat it in a special way, too.

How can we make our church a good place to be for worship, learning, and friendship?

In the pictures at the right, draw in the missing parts. They are things that would help our church (God's house) be a special place.

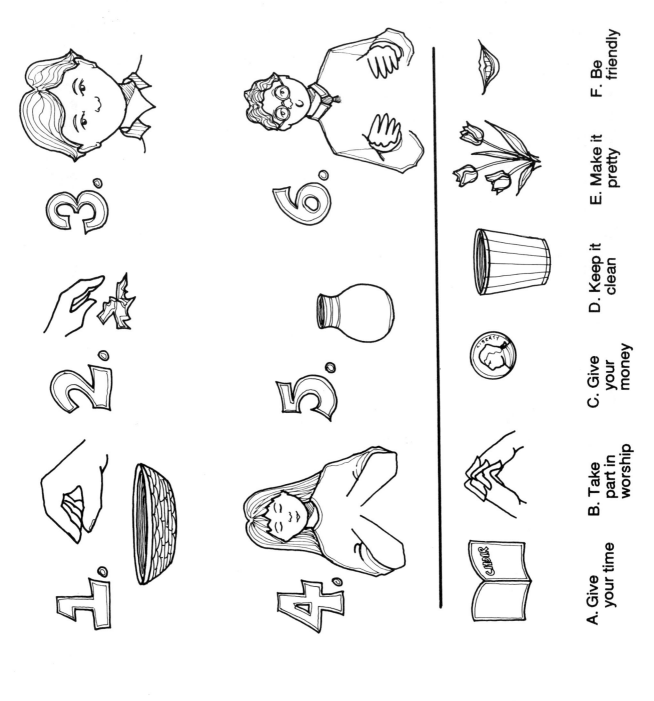

1.

2.

3.

4.

5.

6.

A. Give your time

B. Take part in worship

C. Give your money

D. Keep it clean

E. Make it pretty

F. Be friendly

On this page draw something you like about church.

Music is important at our church. Pay attention to our music today and do the following:

1. **Print this word.**

   HYMN
   _____

   A hymn is a song of praise to God.
   _____

2. **Find each hymn we will be singing today and do your best to sing along.**

3. **Count the number of times the choir sings.**

   _____

4. **Circle the kinds of instruments that are played in church today.**

   guitar   piano   bells

   organ   violin   flute

5. **Does the choir do something special today? What is it?**

6. **Copy the words from Psalm 147:1a and 149:1a on these lines**

1. _____
2. _____
3. _____
4. _____
5. _____

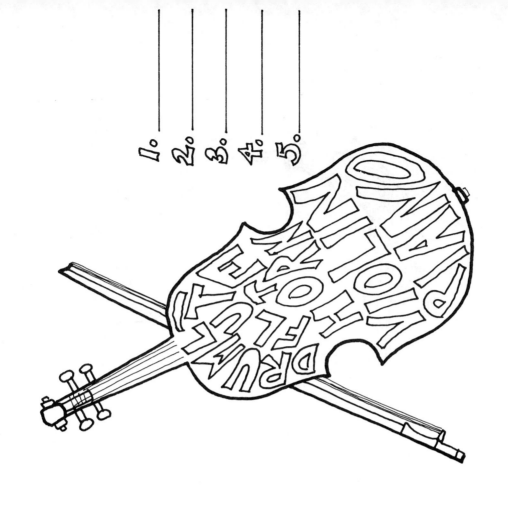

Can you find 5 musical instruments hidden in this picture?

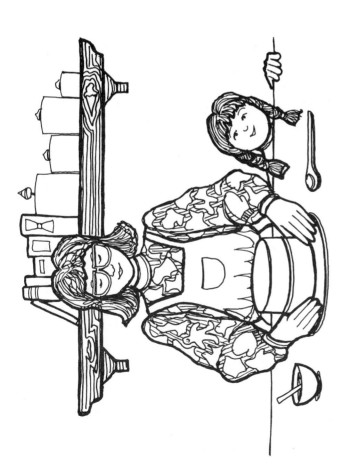

See if you can find a bow, sailboat, mittens, ice cream cone, top, and a gingerbread man hidden in this picture. Then color it and decorate the cake.

A Family Experience:
Try a family hug today! It's easy to hug one person but try to get everyone together for one big hug. Watch out, there should be lots of smiles!

Draw a picture of your super dad.

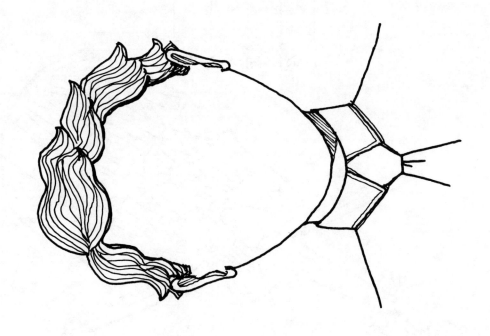

Make a card or picture for Dad.
Fill it with love and don't forget to sign it!

HIDDEN MESSAGE

Color in the squares that have an "X" in the corner. Put the remaining letters on the lines below to find a command that we should practice every day.

N	A	O	T	T	N	H	D	E	L	D	O	T
S	C	V	O	E	L	Y	O	O	R	U	R	
I	N	T	H	E	E	I	E	G	X	E	S	
F	H	B	O	R	A	O	S	R	Y	A	O	U
M	E	S	S	R	S	E	A	L	F	G	E	Q

" ___ ___ ___ ___ ___ ___ ___ ___ ___ ___ ___ ___ ___ ___."

Matthew 19:19

Signs:

What / Walk / Wish

Nose / Note / Not

To / Tell

Open / Others / Once

Don't / Dart / Dew

That / Tail / Take

Before / Belongs / Because

Look at the words in the signs. Write the word that:

1. begins with D and ends with o. _____

2. begins with N and ends with t. _____

3. begins with T and ends with e. _____

4. begins with W and ends with t. _____

5. begins with B and ends with s. _____

6. begins with T and ends with o. _____

7. begins with O and ends with s. _____

Draw a line to the biblical occupation of each person listed below.

CARPENTER	AARON
FISHERMAN	AMOS
KING	AQUILA
MISSIONARY	DAVID
PHYSICIAN	ESTHER
PRIEST	JOSEPH
PROPHET	LUKE
QUEEN	LYDIA
SELLER OF PURPLE	MALCHUS
SERVANT	MATTHEW
SHEPHERD	PAUL
TAX COLLECTOR	PETER
TENTMAKER	SOLOMON

BIBLICAL OCCUPATION WORD FIND
(Use names and occupations listed on the left)

```
Q N E H E M A L C H U S T S U L D T C Y
U A O A M Q S Y O S L A V E U O S E U R
E M D I P R E D N A X E L A R R E H P A
E R R M R S U I C C A P P M V D R P B N
N E E U Q A O P R A I N A D V O E O
R H H E I T L P U M N L V D M A R A I
E S P E S L L N P H Y S I C I A N P R S
K I E N T E V F E S C D H A V T T R E S
A F H E C N O D R C A R P E N T E R R I
M E S T O R J O S E P H L U A H G I E M
T Z O R E O A R M S T H U N T E R N B A
N R A L A C L E I N A D K S E W A K I N
E A L I U Q A U T S I L E G N A V E R K
T E N A A M A N H A N A N A M S D R E H C S
S R E T E P S U M I S E N O M O L O S O
```

JESUS SAID:

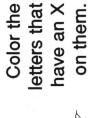

Color the letters that have an X on them.

John 15:5

YOU ARE THE

___ ___ ___ ___ ___

Use the code to write the correct letter on each line.

 R
 B
 H
 N
 A
 C
 E
 S

TWO GREAT RULES

Crack the code to discover the two rules Jesus said were the most important to follow.

1 ___ ___ ___ ___

___ ___ ___ ___

2 ___ ___ ___ ___ ___ ___ ___ ___ ___

___ ___ ___ ___ ___ ___ ___

⊙	◎	⊘	⊛	⊜	⊖	⊗	◉	⊚	⊕
B	D	E	G	H	I	L	N	O	R	U	V	Y

CHILDREN'S BULLETIN

Today Is
Church School
Award Sunday

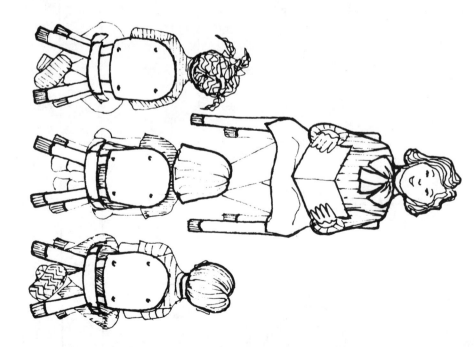

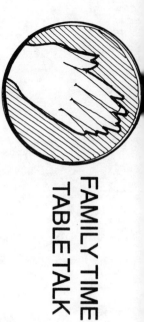

FAMILY TIME
TABLE TALK

1. Thank God for our Church School teachers.
2. Pray for moms and dads in your prayers.
3. Read 1 Samuel 1:3–11 and 19–20 about a very special mother.

This puzzle is about an Old Testament prophet. Put the first letter of each clue in the space to find his name.

___ To live we must ___ food.

___ God so ___ the world.

___ ___ am the light of the world.

___ The walls of ___ fell down.

___ A good red fruit is an ___.

___ It's fun to sing ___ Birthday.

The Last Supper

$\overline{67}\ \overline{96}\ \overline{15}\ \overline{48}\qquad \overline{83}\ \overline{25}\qquad \overline{15}\ \overline{55}$

$\overline{6}\ \overline{3}\ \overline{10}\ \overline{3}\qquad \overline{68}\ \overline{6}\ \overline{77}\qquad \overline{55}\ \overline{39}\ \overline{3}$

$\overline{25}\ \overline{35}\qquad \overline{10}\ \overline{3}$ '

O	C	E	B
15 +10	32 +7	20 -17	56 +12

H	M	I	S
84 +12	72 -62	45 -30	36 +12

T	N	A	R
94 -27	33 +22	30 +47	58 -52

D	F		
98 -15	17 +18		

Solve the puzzle by first doing the math problems. Then put the letter on the blanks above.

Lord's Supper

This morning we celebrate the Lord's Supper. This helps remind us of Jesus' sacrifice when He died for us. The Mystery Picture will be of something that also reminds us of His death. To finish the picture, pick the correct answer to each question. Color in the square that has the same number as your answer. (The first one is done for you.)

Mystery Picture

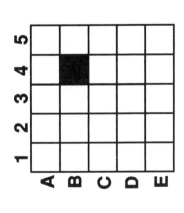

1. During Communion the wine is a sign of:
   A-2 running water
   B-4 Jesus' blood

2. The bread is a sign of:
   E-3 Jesus' body
   D-1 the wheat harvest

3. During Communion we remember:
   A-5 Jesus' birth
   B-3 Jesus' death

4. To take Communion we must:
   D-5 be perfect
   D-3 be sorry for our sins

5. We also remember that:
   A-3 our sins are forgiven
   C-4 Moses gave us the Law

6. When Jesus celebrated the first Lord's Supper, He was with:
   C-2 His family
   B-2 His disciples

7. Jesus' death paid for:
   B-5 His sins
   C-3 our sins

Draw a picture of the communion table up front.

Find a nine-letter word telling about the Lord's Supper (hidden in this picture).

The Greek word *koinonia* (pronounced coin-a-neya) means communion, or fellowship.

Our growing minds and spirits

Many things help us to grow. Find these words in the puzzle below.

Catechism
Sunday School
Parents
Teachers
Bible

Preachers
Church
Prayer
School
Sermons

```
A C P P D G D H L J N Z T
P A R E N T S Q V R A I S
R Q A C A L V I N E T T E
E H Y N F Y M B I L S G N
A T E A C H E R S B E N C
C X R G L A K A R I J I H
H C A D E T N C I B U W U
E C A T E C H I S M P O R
R L W S C H O O L D E R C
S E R M O N S T V O O G H
I L O O H C S Y A D N U S
```

gROWING in God's family

Look up 2 Peter 3:18 on page _____ in your Bible and fill in the blanks.

"B__ t gr__w __ n th__ __

gr__c__ __ __ __ nd

kn__wl__dg__ __ f

__ __ r L__ rd __ nd

S__ v__ __ r J__ s__ s

Chr__ st."

+ − ○ △ □
a e i o u

Complete the maze by starting at the dot and finishing at the square.

THINKERS ONLY!!

How many books of the Bible can you name that rhyme with these words?

1. Truth _____
2. Spaniel _____
3. Brings _____
4. Neater _____
5. Jester _____
6. Famous _____
7. Calms _____

Bible Families

How well do you know parents and children in the Bible? On the left are listed Biblical fathers and mothers. On the right are listed one child of each parent. Draw a line from the parent to the child.

1. Eve   Absalom
2. Noah   Samuel
3. David   Cain
4. Saul   Isaac
5. Abraham   David
6. Rebekah   Ham
7. Hannah   Jonathan
8. Jesse   Jacob

A New Year—
see it in with God!

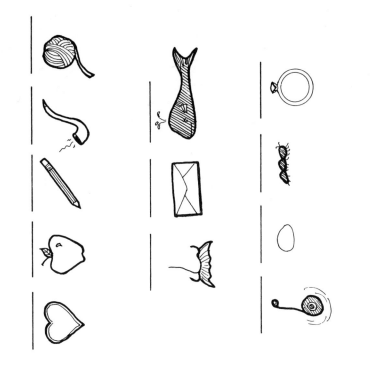

Put the first letter of the object below the line **ON** that line.

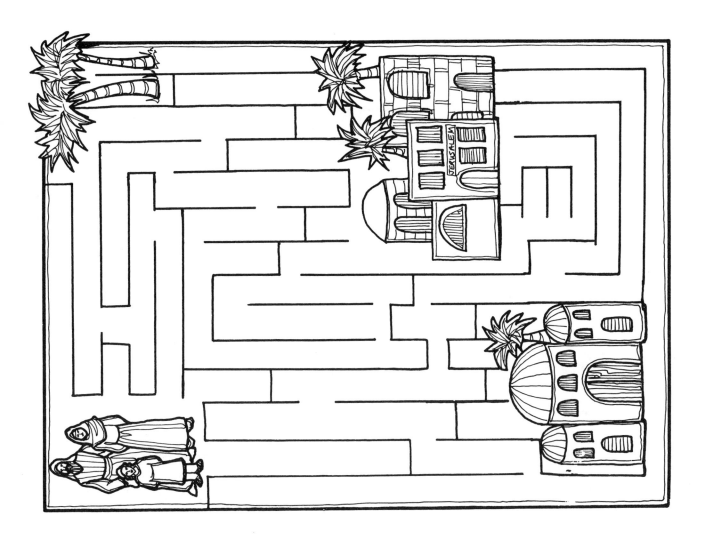

Find your way through the maze to
make a special message. Write
each letter below as you come to it.

START

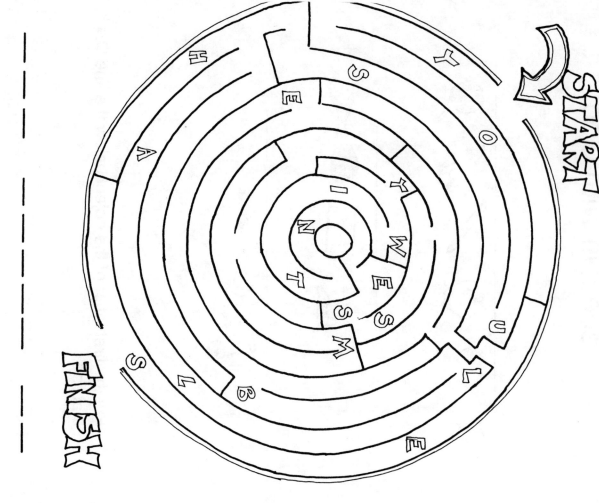

FINISH

_ _ _ _ _ _ _ _ _ _ _ _ _ _ _

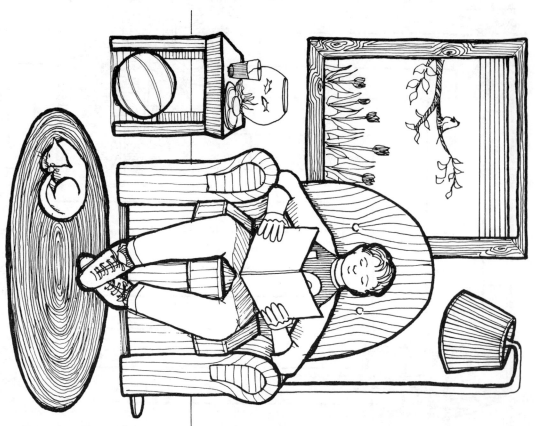

God gives many things to us. Find 10 things
that you've been given. List three things that
you can give to God.

1. _____

2. _____

3. _____

1= red
2= black
3= green
4= yellow
5= blue
6= brown

1= pink
2= green
3= brown
4= yellow
5= orange
6= white
7= black
8= blue

Read the verses Martin Luther found in the Bible by decoding this puzzle.

Unscramble these books of the Bible to see what books this text are found in . . . .

KUABKAHK _____

ASOMRN _____

TSALAAGNI _____

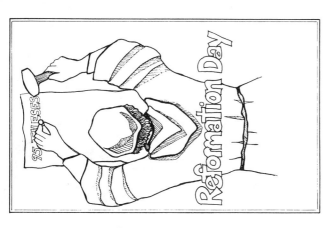

Ma___tin Luther struggled ___very day trying to ___ind peace for his s___ul. While studying the Bible, he ___ead, "The just shall live by faith." Suddenly free from the chains of works, ___artin began to pre___ch the ___ruths ___n God's Word. On ___ctober 31, 1517 he ___ailed 95 thesis to the door of his church.

Use the letters of our special day to fill in the blanks. Put R in the first blank, and so on.

Draw a line to the matching picture.

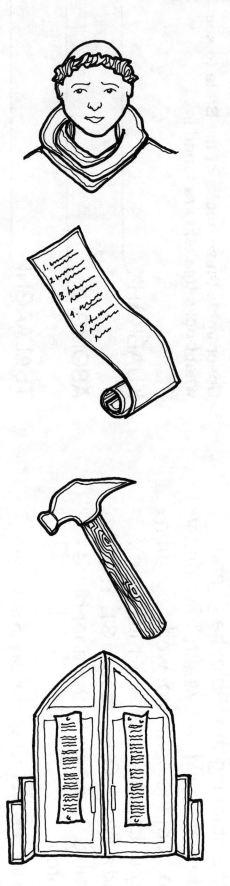

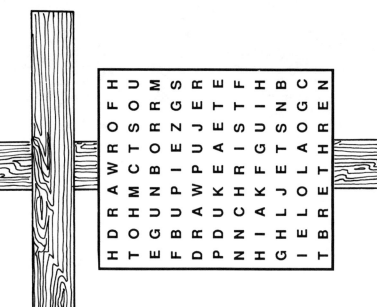

H	D	R	A	W	R	O	F	H
T	O	H	M	C	T	S	O	U
E	G	U	N	B	O	R	R	M
F	B	U	P	I	E	Z	G	S
D	R	A	W	P	U	J	E	R
P	D	U	K	E	A	E	T	E
N	N	C	H	R	I	S	T	F
H	I	A	K	F	G	U	I	H
G	H	L	J	E	T	S	N	B
I	E	L	O	L	A	O	G	C
T	B	R	E	T	H	R	E	N

Find the underlined words

"<u>Brethren</u>, I do not consider that I have made it my own; but one thing I do, <u>forgetting</u> what lies <u>behind</u> and straining <u>forward</u> to what lies ahead, I press on toward the <u>goal</u> for the prize of the <u>upward call</u> of <u>God</u> in <u>Christ Jesus</u>."

Philippians 3:13-14 (RSV)

FAITH IN JESUS

DESIGN YOUR OWN CROSS

The Cross is the most popular symbol of the Christian faith. It has been used by Christians through the ages to remind us of how Jesus brought us life through death on a cross. There are many different kinds of crosses. Below are four samples.

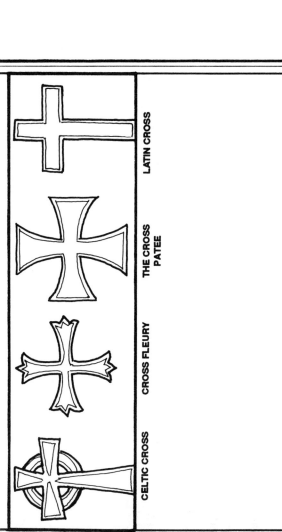

CELTIC CROSS   CROSS FLEURY   THE CROSS PATEE   LATIN CROSS

Use the space above to design a cross.

For the Very Young

KEEP MY COMMANDMENTS

EXODUS 20:6

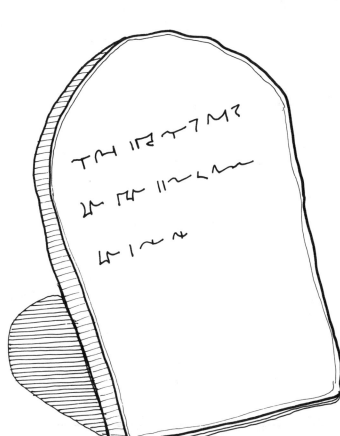
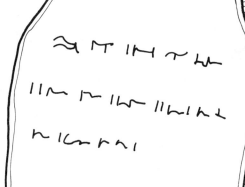

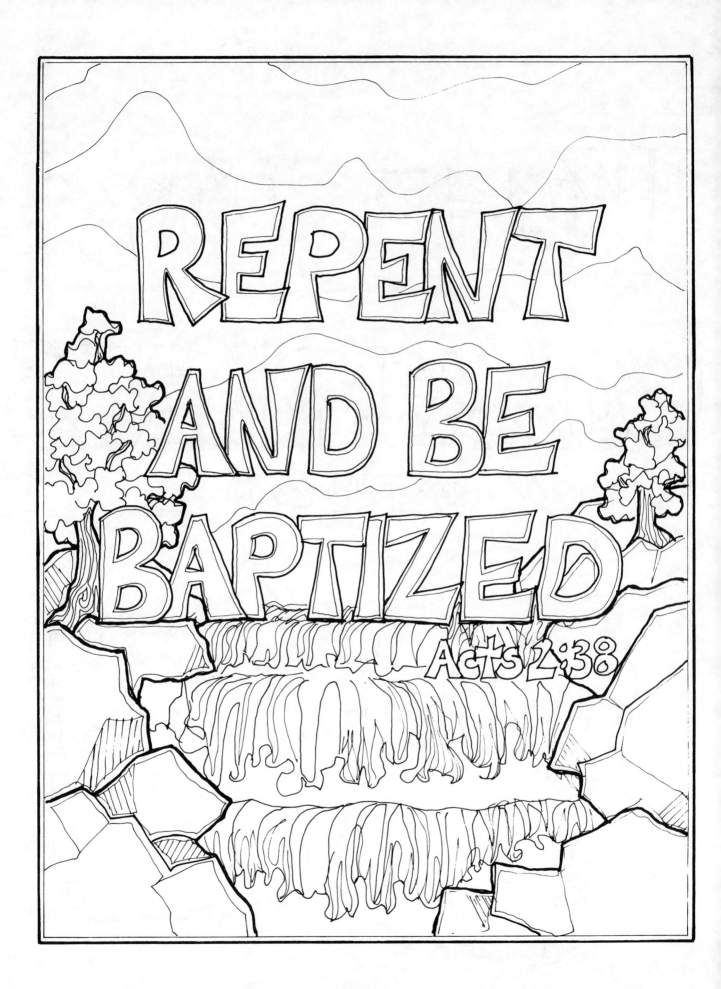

MATTHEW 3:17 KJV

THIS IS MY BELOVED SON IN WHOM I AM WELL PLEASED

TEN
COMMANDMENTS

13

9

14

10

12

8

15

11

7

16

1

17

20 2

5

18

19 3

1

Go tell it on the mountains!

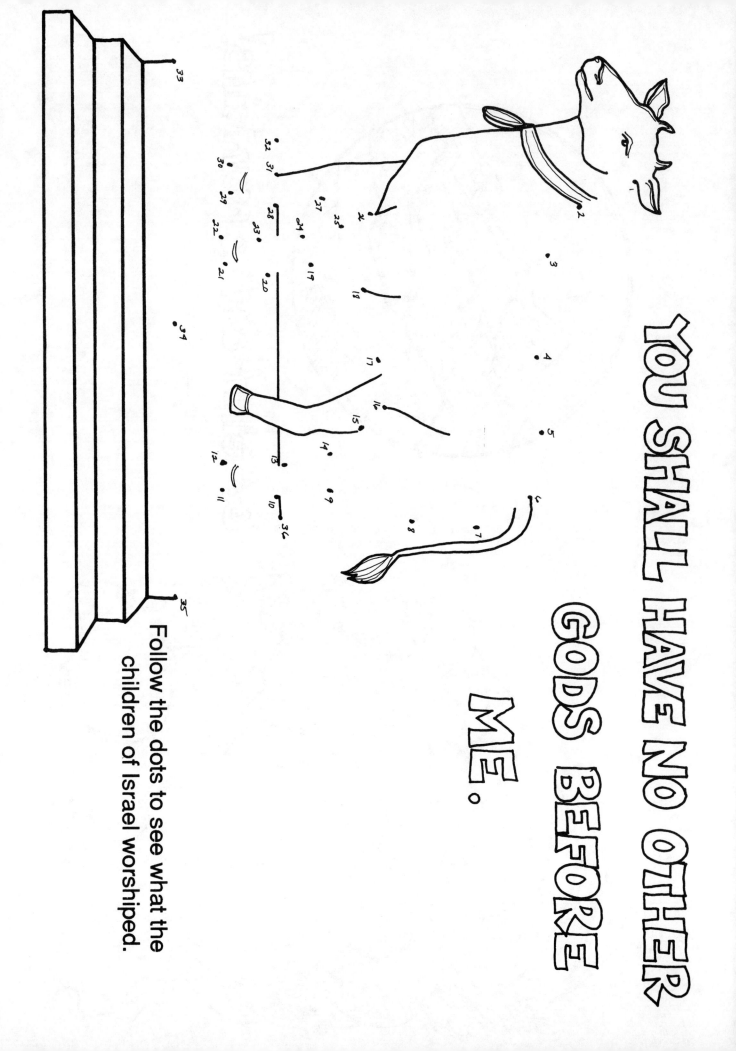

YOU SHALL HAVE NO OTHER GODS BEFORE ME.

Follow the dots to see what the children of Israel worshiped.

We bring our offerings to God as a way
of showing Him we love Him.

Draw some money in the offering plate.

Dear Jesus, I bring my gift to You,
because I love You. Amen.

When people die we feel sad, but we can feel happy too, because they can live in heaven with Jesus.

Draw a face on John the way you think he feels.

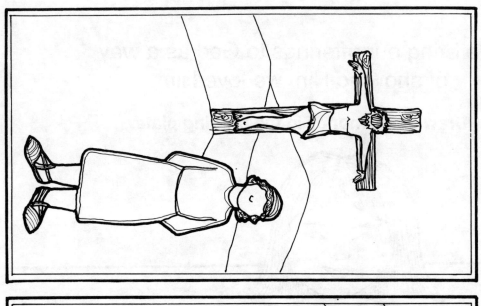

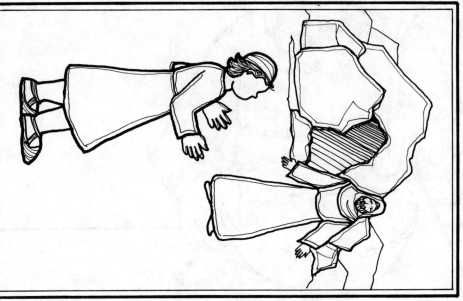

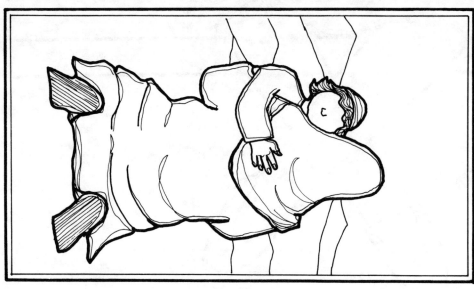

Things that make us think about Jesus

Draw a line to match the objects.

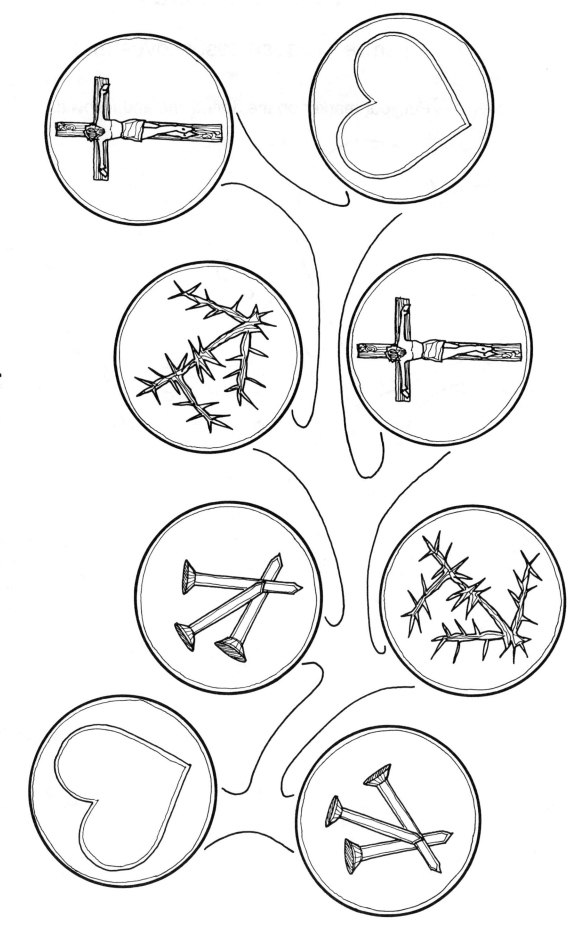

Valentine's Day

I smile because Jesus loves me!

Put your marker on the dotted line and follow it.

Find the road to the Land of Canaan.

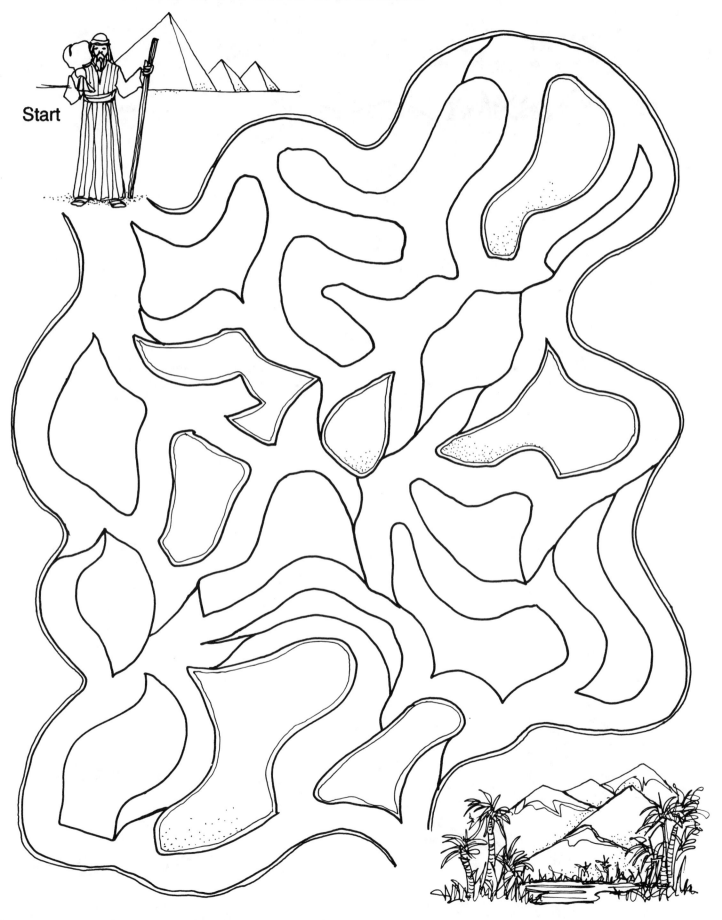

Start

Palm Sunday

Complete the dotted picture and you will see the animal that Jesus rode on Palm Sunday.

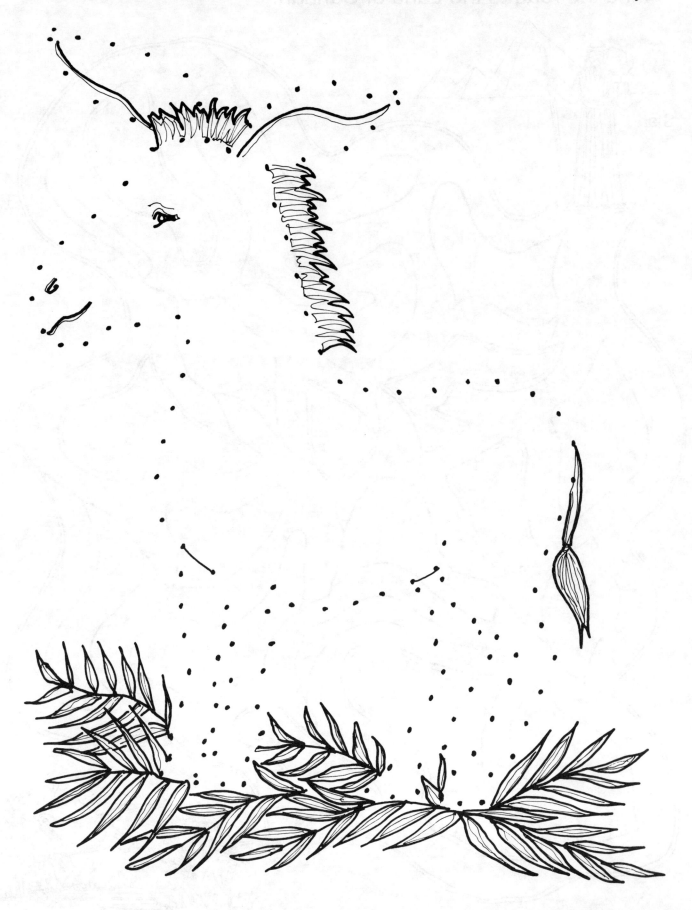

Thank You, God, for the food we eat. Amen.

Place your marker on the object, then follow the line to the food.

This do in remembrance of me.

Follow the line to find a matching object.

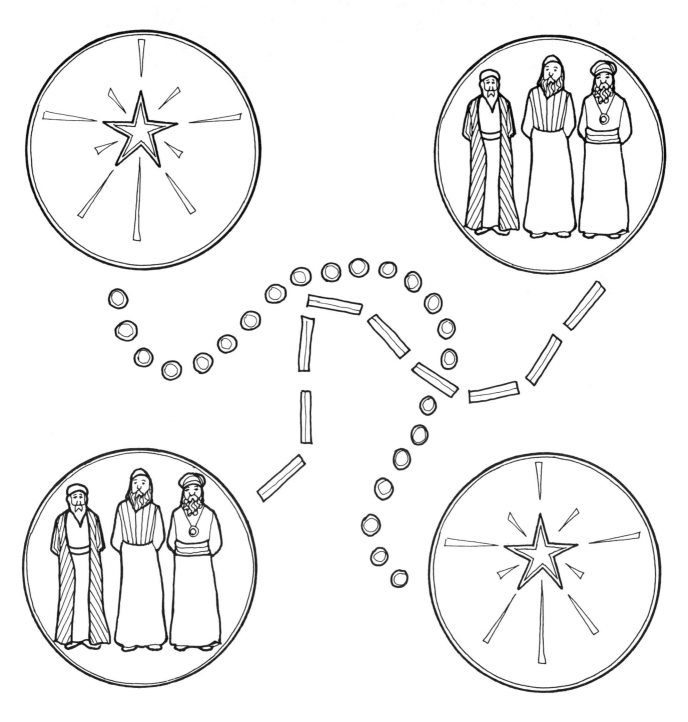

The wise men followed a star to find the baby Jesus.

Draw a circle around each child who is hiding in the picture.

We can hide from each other, but we can't hide from God!

Art, Headings, Borders

CHILDREN'S BULLETIN CHILDREN'S BULLETIN CHILDREN'S BULLETIN CHILDREN'S BULLETIN CHILDREN'S BULLETIN CHILDREN'S BULLETIN CHILDREN'S BULLETIN CHILDREN'S BULLETIN CHILDREN'S BULLETIN CHILDREN'S BULLETIN CHILDREN'S BULLETIN CHILDREN'S BULLETIN CHILDREN'S BULLETIN

CHILDREN'S BULLETIN CHILDREN'S BULLETIN CHILDREN'S BULLETIN CHILDREN'S BULLETIN CHILDREN'S BULLETIN CHILDREN'S BULLETIN CHILDREN'S BULLETIN CHILDREN'S BULLETIN CHILDREN'S BULLETIN CHILDREN'S BULLETIN CHILDREN'S BULLETIN CHILDREN'S BULLETIN CHILDREN'S BULLETIN

CHILDREN'S BULLETIN CHILDREN'S BULLETIN CHILDREN'S BULLETIN CHILDREN'S BULLETIN CHILDREN'S BULLETIN CHILDREN'S BULLETIN CHILDREN'S BULLETIN CHILDREN'S BULLETIN CHILDREN'S BULLETIN CHILDREN'S BULLETIN CHILDREN'S BULLETIN CHILDREN'S BULLETIN CHILDREN'S BULLETIN

CHILDREN'S BULLETIN CHILDREN'S BULLETIN CHILDREN'S BULLETIN CHILDREN'S BULLETIN CHILDREN'S BULLETIN CHILDREN'S BULLETIN CHILDREN'S BULLETIN CHILDREN'S BULLETIN CHILDREN'S BULLETIN CHILDREN'S BULLETIN CHILDREN'S BULLETIN CHILDREN'S BULLETIN CHILDREN'S BULLETIN

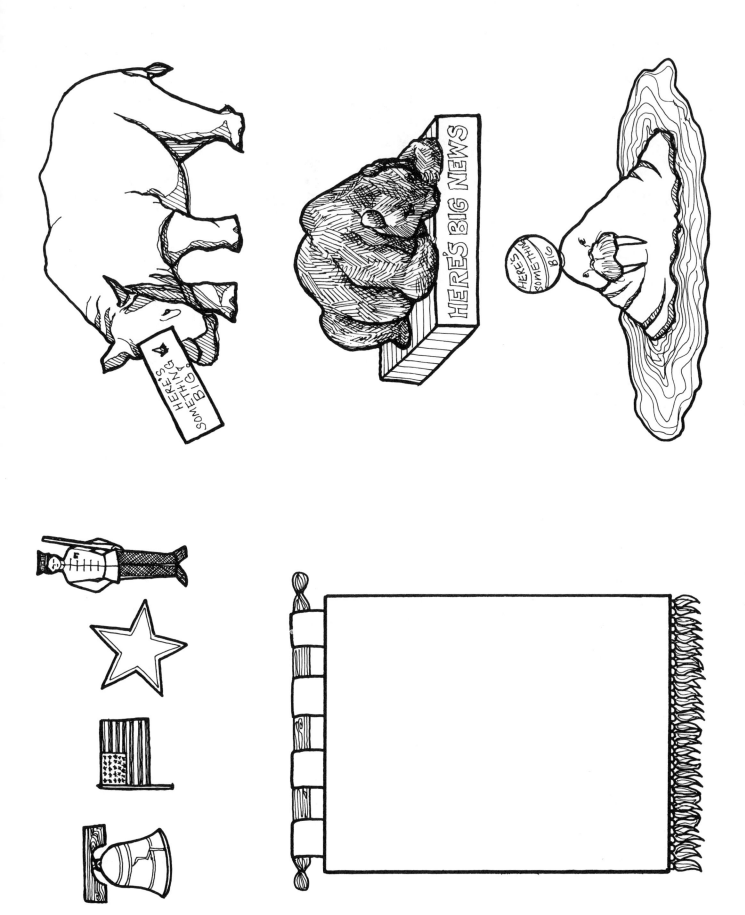

CHRISTMAS

GOOD FRIDAY

THANKSGIVING DAY

HAPPY BIRTHDAY AMERICA

ALL NATIONS

HERITAGE DAY

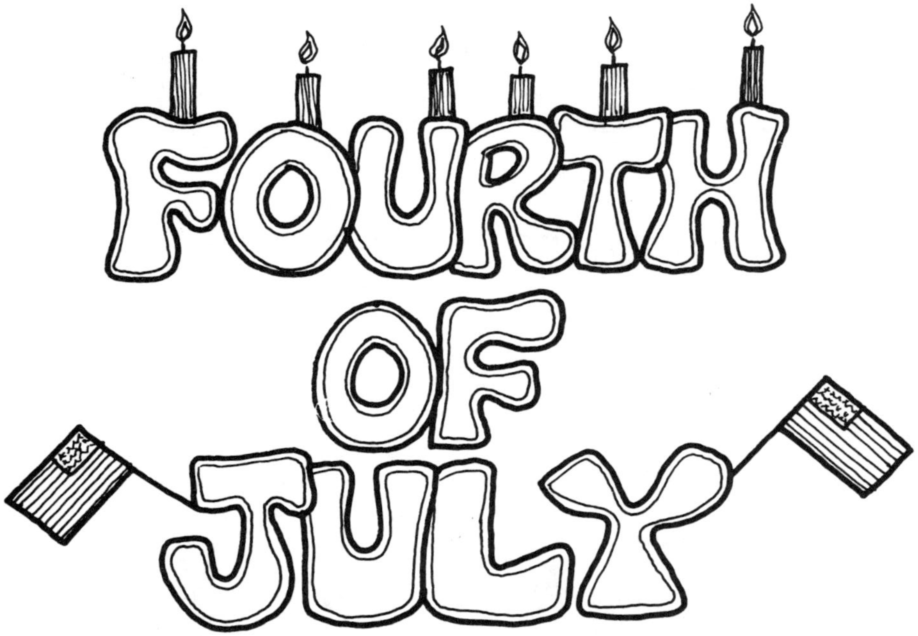

FOURTH OF JULY

ADVENT

FIRST WEEK:

ADVENT

SECOND WEEK:

ADVENT

THIRD WEEK:

ADVENT

FOURTH WEEK:

MUSIC SOCIAL STUDIES BIBLE MATH HISTORY ART SPELLING ENGLISH

BACK TO SCHOOL

BACK TO SCHOOL

World Hunger Day

Disability Awareness Sunday

Hunger Awareness Week

World Hunger Week Bible Bible Sunday

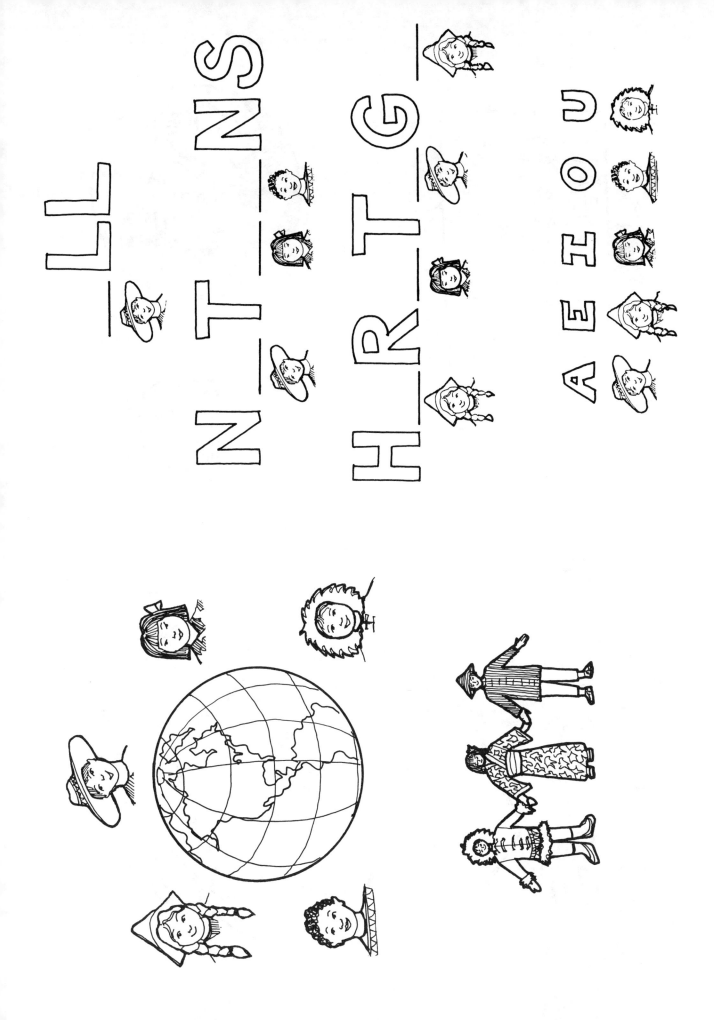

We're glad you're part of God's Family. WELCOME!

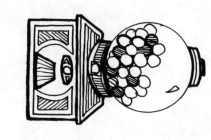

GOD CARES FOR HIS WORLD

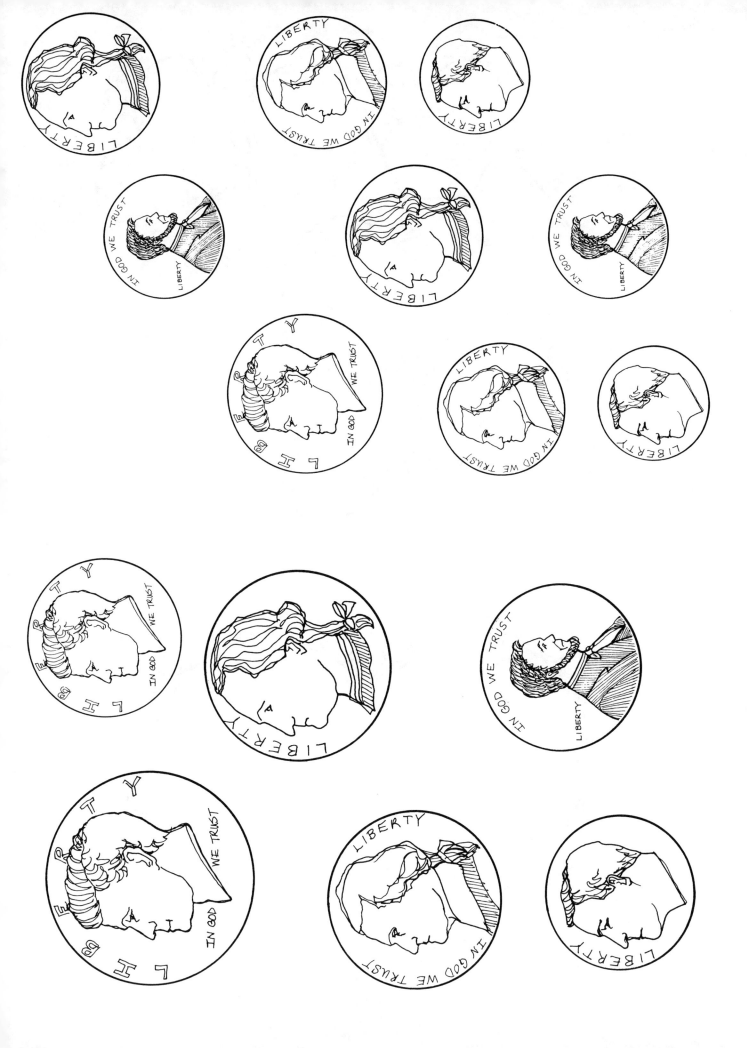

CHILDREN'S BULLETIN

CHILDREN'S BULLETIN

CHILDREN'S BULLETIN

CHILDREN'S BULLETIN

CHILDREN'S BULLETIN

CHILDREN'S BULLETIN

FAMILY TIME TABLE TALK

KNOW YOUR CHURCH FAMILY

MYSTERY PERSON

MISSION

EMPHASIS WEEK

Happy Birthday!

HAPPY MOTHER'S DAY

HAPPY FATHER'S DAY

BULLETIN BOARD

LABOR DAY

EASTER

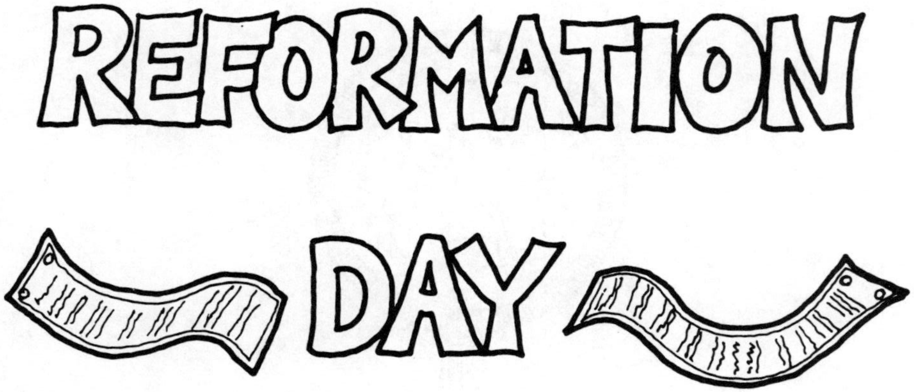

MEMORIAL DAY

REFORMATION DAY

PENTECOST

ASCENSION DAY

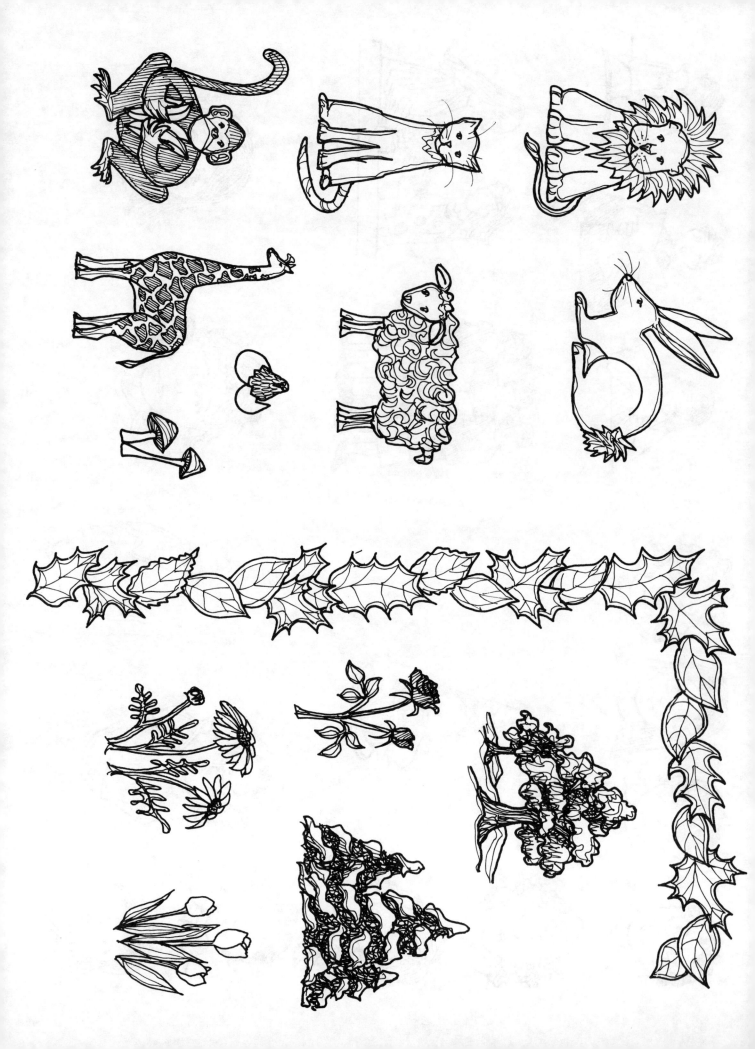

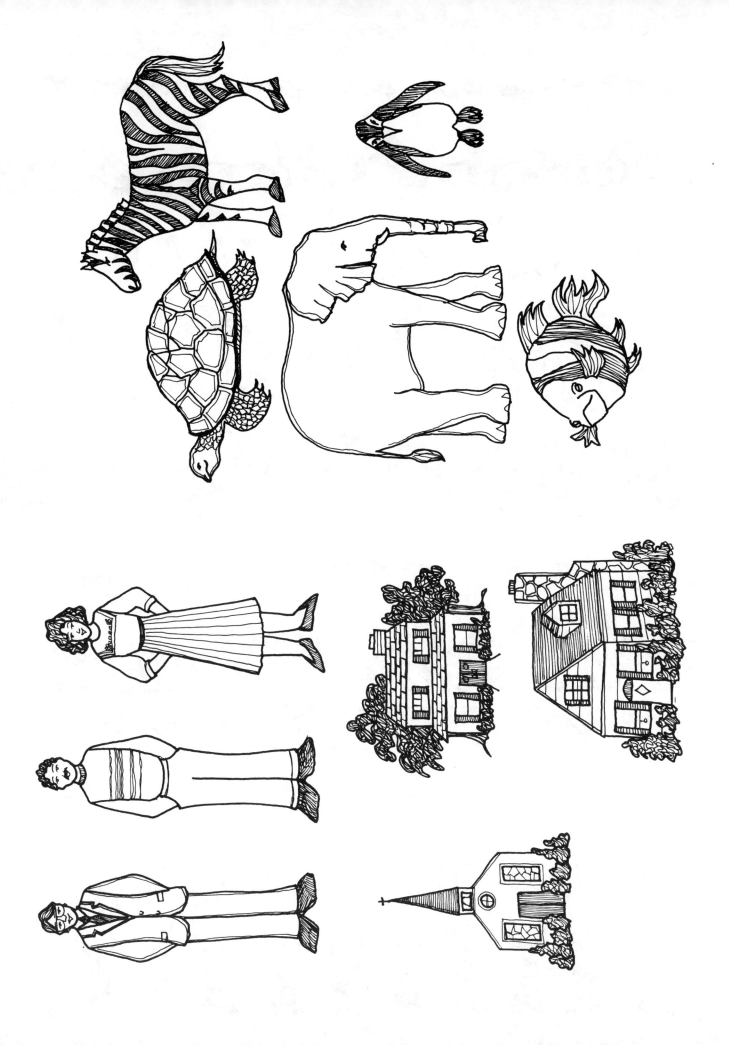

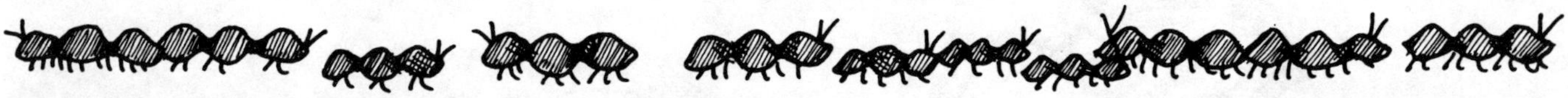
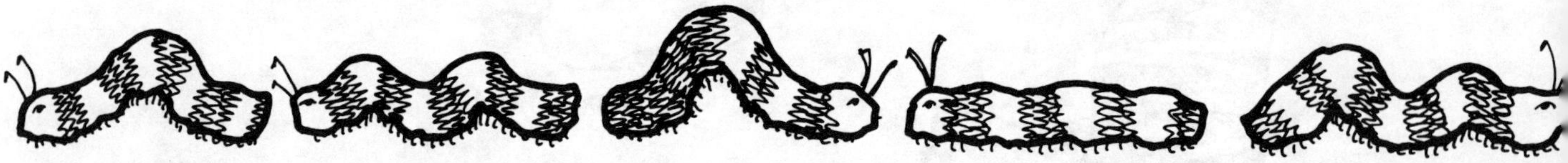
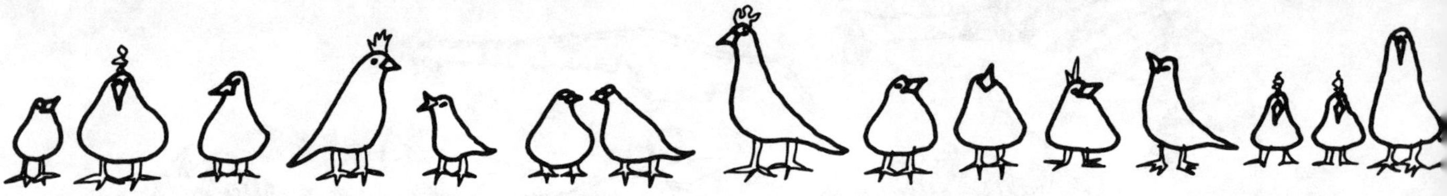
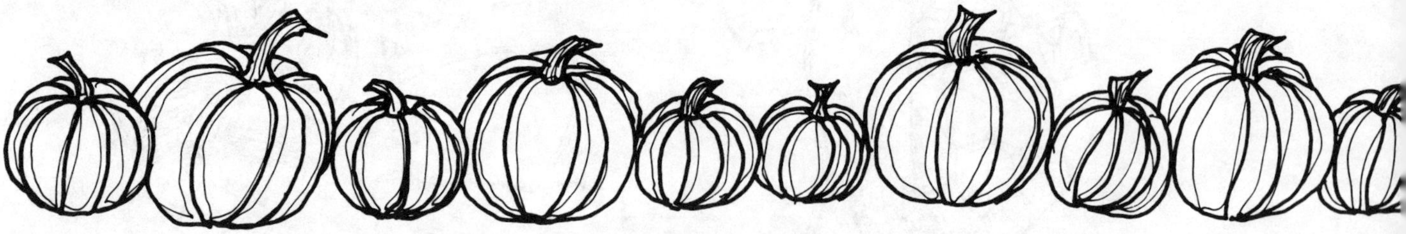
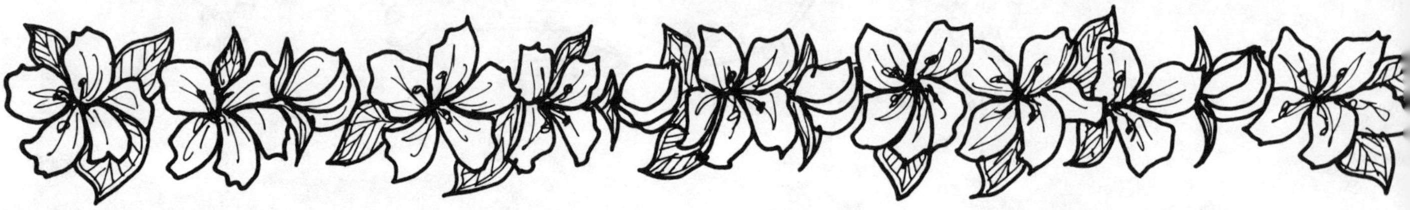
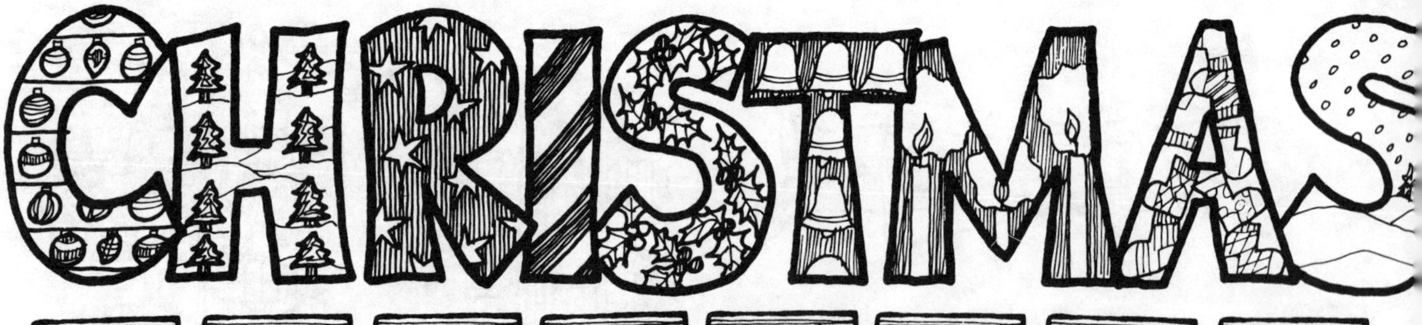
CHRISTMAS
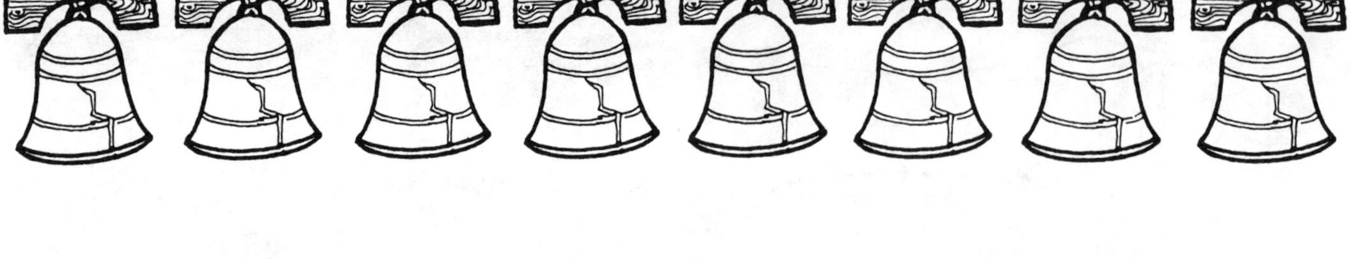
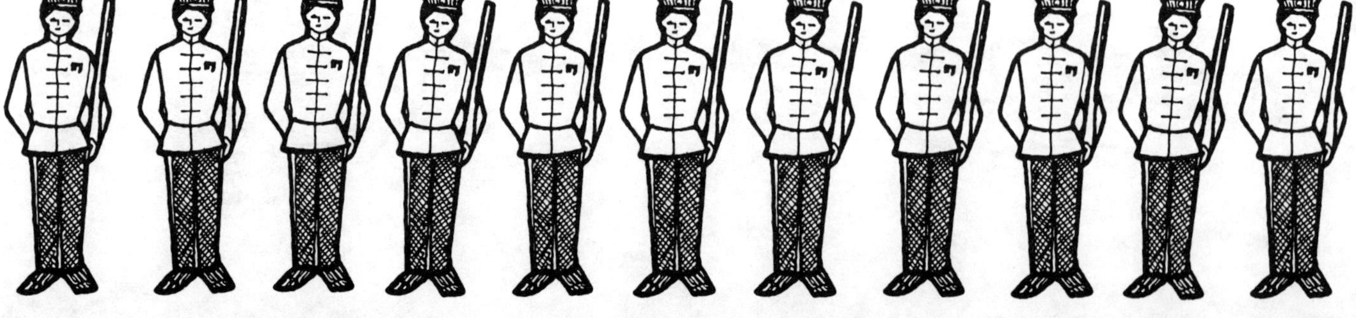

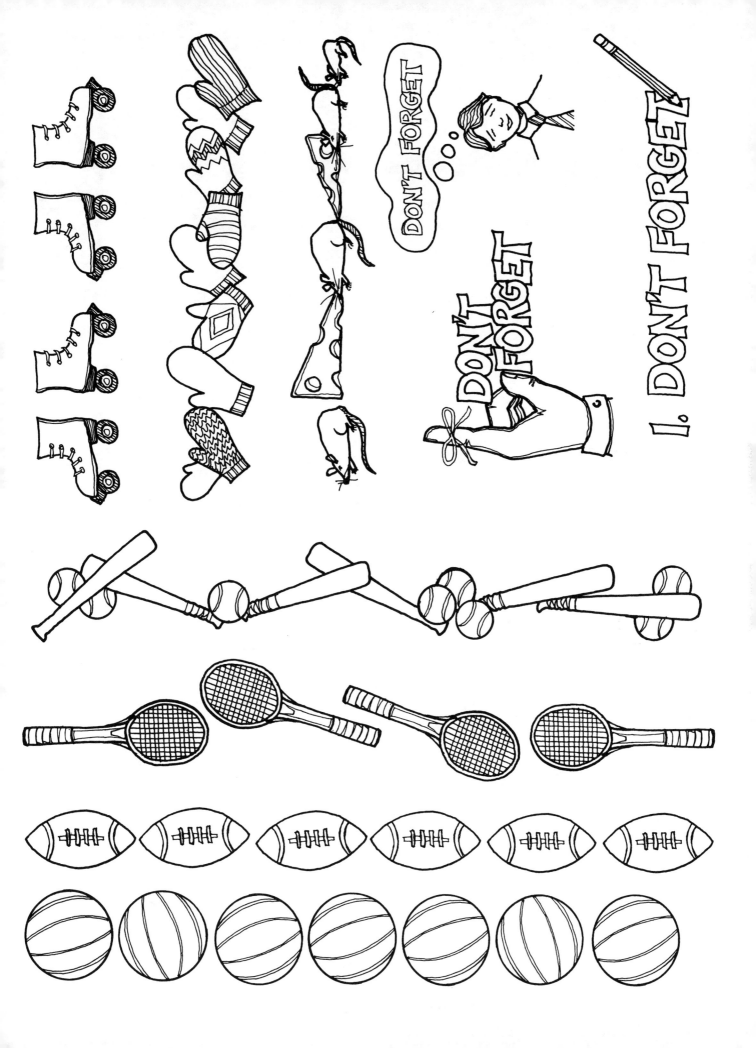